Exploring **C**anada

QUEBEC

Titles in the Exploring Canada series include:

Alberta

British Columbia

Manitoba

Ontario

Yukon Territory

Exploring Canada

QUEBEC

by Steven Ferry

LUCENT
BOOKS®

THOMSON
──★──™
GALE

San Diego • Detroit • New York • San Francisco • Cleveland • New Haven, Conn. • Waterville, Maine • London • Munich

Development, management, design, and composition by Pre-Press Company, Inc.

© 2003 by Lucent Books. Lucent Books is an imprint of The Gale Group, Inc.,
a division of Thomson Learning, Inc.

Lucent Books® and Thomson Learning™ are trademarks used herein under license.

For more information, contact
Lucent Books
27500 Drake Rd.
Farmington Hills, MI 48331-3535
Or you can visit our Internet site at http://www.gale.com

LIBRARY OF CONGRESS CATALOGING-IN-PUBLICATION DATA

Ferry, Steven, 1953–
    Quebec / by Steven Ferry.
        p. cm. — (Exploring Canada series)
    Summary: Examines the history, geography, climate, industries, people,
    culture, and ongoing separatist struggle of Canada's largest province.
    Includes bibliographical references and index.
        ISBN 1-59018-051-8 (hardback : alk. paper).
        1. Quâebec (Province)—Juvenile literature. 2. Quâebec (Province)—History—
    Juvenile literature. [1. Quâebec (Province) 2. Canada.]   I. Title.   II. Series.
        F1052.4 .F47 2003
        971.4—dc21   2002004111

Printed in the United States of America

Contents

Foreword.

Any truly accurate portrait of Canada would have to be painted in sharp contrasts, for this is a long-inhabited but only recently settled land. It is a vast and expansive region peopled by a predominantly urban population. Canada is also a nation of natives and immigrants that, as its Prime Minister Lester Pearson remarked in the late 1960s, has "not yet found a Canadian soul except in time of war." Perhaps it is in these very contrasts that this elusive national identity is waiting to be found.

Canada as an inhabited place is among the oldest in the Western Hemisphere, having accepted prehistoric migrants more than eleven thousand years ago after they crossed a land bridge where the Bering Strait now separates Alaska from Siberia. Canada is also the site of the New World's earliest European settlement, L'Anse aux Meadows on the northern tip of Newfoundland Island. A band of Vikings lived there briefly some five hundred years before Columbus reached the West Indies in 1492.

Yet as a nation Canada is still a relative youngster on the world scene. It gained its independence almost a century after the American Revolution and half a century after the wave of nationalist uprisings in South America. Canada did not include Newfoundland until 1949 and could not amend its own constitution without approval from the British Parliament until 1982. "The Sleeping Giant," as Canada is sometimes known, came within a whisker of losing a province in 1995, when the people of Quebec narrowly voted down an independence referendum.

In 1999 Canada carved out a new territory, Nunavut, which has a population equal to that of Key West, Florida, spread over an area the size of Alaska and California combined.

As the second-largest country in the world (after Russia), the land itself is also famously diverse. British Columbia's "Pocket Desert" near the town of Osoyoos is the northernmost desert in North America. A few hundred miles away, in Alberta's Banff National Park, one can walk on the Columbia Icefields, the largest nonpolar icecap in the world. In parts of Manitoba and the Yukon glacially created sand dunes creep slowly across the landscape. Quebec and Ontario have so many lakes in the boundless north that tens of thousands remain unnamed.

One can only marvel at a place where the contrasts range from the profound (the first medical use of insulin) to the mundane (the invention of Trivial Pursuit); the sublime (the poetry of Ontario-born Robertson Davies) to the ridiculous (the comic antics of Ontario-born Jim Carrey); the British (ever-so-quaint Victoria) to the French (Montreal, the world's second-largest French-speaking city); and the environmental (Greenpeace was founded in Vancouver) to the industrial (refuse from nickel mining near Sudbury, Ontario, left a landscape so barren that American astronauts used it to train for their moon walks).

Given these contrasts and conflicts, can this national experiment known as Canada survive? Or to put it another way, what is it that unites as Canadians the elderly Inuit woman selling native crafts in the Yukon; the millionaire businessman-turned-restaurateur recently emigrated from Hong Kong to Vancouver; the mixed-French (Métis) teenager living in a rural settlement in Manitoba; the cosmopolitan French-speaking professor of archeology in Quebec City; and the raw-boned Nova Scotia fisherman struggling to make a living? These are questions only Canadians can answer, and perhaps will have to face for many decades.

A true portrait of Canada can't, therefore, be provided by a brief essay, any more than a snapshot captures the entire life of a centenarian. But the Exploring Canada series can offer an illuminating overview of individual provinces and territories. Each book smartly summarizes an area's geography, history, arts and culture, daily life, and contemporary issues. Read individually or as a series, they show that what Canadians undeniably have in common is a shared heritage as people who came, whether in past millennia or last year, to a land with a difficult climate and a challenging geography, yet somehow survived and worked with one another to form a vibrant whole.

What Is Quebec?

How does one describe the largest of Canada's provinces, one in which three countries the size of France would fit, or one American state the size of Texas with room to spare? A quarter of Canada's population calls Quebec home, as well as most of its Francophones (people who speak French). With eight in every ten residents of Quebec speaking their native French, a casual visitor might feel tempted to conclude the province is an outpost of France. And they may not be far from the truth.

Four centuries ago, French explorers and colonists landed along the eastern shore of what is now Canada. At first the new arrivals adopted parts of the culture of the natives living there, but soon their own French culture dominated, with buildings, fashions, beliefs, tools, and clothing becoming a mirror image of their old homeland across the ocean.

When the British took control of Canada in the mid-1700s, most English colonists settled in the area just west of Quebec, now known as Ontario, and the few who settled in Quebec learned to follow the French majority. The British leaders, anyway, admired the French culture, so assimilation was not a difficult choice. The wave of Americans loyal to the British crown who emigrated to Canada after the American War of Independence also mostly settled in Ontario, though some found new homes in Quebec.

For more than three centuries, it has been clear that the French-speaking Canadians in Quebec like their culture and

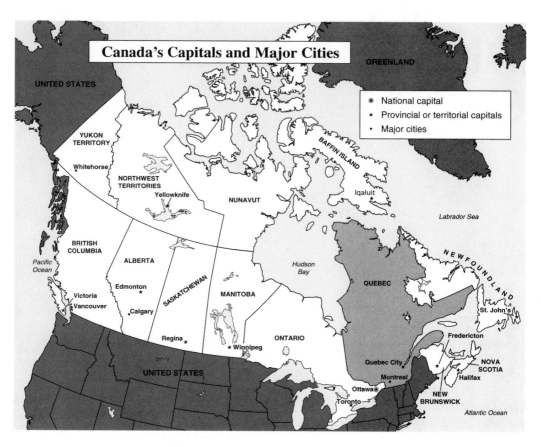

Canada's Capitals and Major Cities

they want to keep it. Wedged between the American culture to the south and the non-French-speaking Canadian culture to Quebec's east and west, the Quebecers have recently become more vocal about protecting their language and culture, even at times talking of separating from the rest of Canada.

But as much as the French-speaking Quebecers (or Quebecois, as they call themselves) protest the invasion of the English culture, the province is still very much French. The French language is spoken everywhere, even in schools. The food and the architecture are distinctly French. Most institutions have some connection to their French origins. All these factors attest to the region's desire to remain attached to its French roots. And that makes Quebec almost unique in North America, where the only other pockets of French culture are to be found in Louisiana, a state where the French heritage has been severely diluted by things and ideas American, and in St. Pierre and Miquelon, two small French islands off the southern coast of Newfoundland.

Today modern travel and communications have strengthened Quebec's contacts with other French cultures and brought

Quebecers much closer to France and their French heritage. During earlier centuries, when it took weeks for a ship to sail across the Atlantic and up several hundred miles of the St. Lawrence River to Montreal, the customs and language of French Canadians grew apart from those of France and became influenced by their native and British neighbors, as well as the entirely different environment they were in. But now French Quebecers see the latest French movies and TV shows; they listen to French orchestras and see French theater performances. Quebecois writers are published in France, and many of Quebec's best students go to France, not Canada, England, or America to obtain advanced degrees.

Although Quebec is closer to France than ever before, the years of isolation have already resulted in key differences, especially in French Canadian speech, which is quite different from the French spoken in France. The language known as "Joual" (derived from the French word *cheval* meaning "horse") is descended from the way the farmers and artisans of Normandy, France, used to speak. Thanks to living with English speakers, anglicized words and phrases have also entered the French Canadian vocabulary, such as *la job* and

■ *Quebec residents relax at a streetside cafe. The province's French origins are evident throughout the region.*

c'est fun ("it is fun"). Plus Canadian French is the only French language to include words for nonmetric measurements, such as *pouce* for "inch" and *pied* for "foot."

These incursions into the region's culture demonstrate how Quebec's identity is both French and not French. Over the centuries it has been influenced by the United States and its predominantly English culture. Ever since Americans won their independence from Britain, Quebecers have resisted being swallowed up by the American culture. This is true even today, as American television programs, radio stations, products, and people flood into Quebec every minute of the day and night.

So what is Quebec, if it isn't American, French, English, or

■ *Quebec City residents enjoy Summerfest, the largest international French event in North America. Quebec's culture is a unique combination of French, American, English, and Canadian influences.*

even, perhaps, Canadian? Quebec, it seems, according to the Quebec government, "is North American by virtue of its geographic location, French in origin and British from the standpoint of its parliamentary system. While it is a French-speaking society, recent waves of immigration are making it increasingly cosmopolitan."[1]

That makes Quebec, well, unique! More than anything else, Quebec is Quebec and the people are not only proud of it, but also determined that their distinctive culture continue. Yet, Quebecers have also worked together to make their province an important contributor to the nation as a whole. Whether people know Quebec through its artists, such as Celine Dion or Cirque du Soleil, or through its products (the province is the ninth largest trading partner for the United States), or its work to preserve the world's environment, they should know one thing about its inhabitants: Over the centuries they have created a unique culture proud of its diverse heritage.

A Rich and Challenging Land

Q uebec is shaped like a giant flint arrowhead pointing south from the Arctic Circle toward the heart of the eastern United States. The province is actually a peninsula, surrounded on three sides by water. The Gulf of St. Lawrence and the St. Lawrence River on the east separate Quebec from the Canadian maritime provinces of New Brunswick, Nova Scotia, Prince Edward Island, and Newfoundland. To the north is the frigid North Atlantic's Hudson Strait. (To the northeast, Quebec borders on remote Labrador, a part of Newfoundland Province.) Even most of the western side of Quebec backs onto the giant Hudson and James Bays, so that the province's only connection to any land other than Labrador is the southwestern border that it shares with Ontario.

Within this vast region, many different peoples have settled over the years, mostly clustered around the rivers and lakes of the more temperate southern areas. While each group has its own unique history and culture, hopes and ambitions, the one reality they have all shared and the hostile force they have had in common is the harsh and unrelenting environment. Each group found a way not only to survive despite the odds, but also to prosper by seizing upon the opportunities the riches of the land offer to those smart enough to recognize them.

An Imposing Terrain

Within the almost 600,000 square miles (1,500,000 square kilometers) that comprise modern-day Quebec lie three distinct

geological regions: the great granite plains of the Canadian Shield in the north; a small section of Appalachian uplands—part of the same ancient and eroded mountain chain that stretches from Alabama to Newfoundland—along the southeast edge of the province; and, squeezed between them, the narrow strip of the St. Lawrence lowlands.

Of the three regions, the Canadian Shield is by far the largest. It covers almost half of Canada and more than 90 percent of Quebec, basically everything west and north of the St. Lawrence River with the exception of the lowlands from Quebec City to south of Montreal. The Shield comprises some of the oldest rock in the world, dating from the Precambrian period more than a billion years ago. The generally flat and exposed terrain is primarily a plateau lying at an altitude of 1,500 to 2,000 feet (460 to 600 meters). Mountain ranges, such as the Laurentians in the south and the Otish Mountains in the center of the province, ripple across the Shield, at some points rising to peaks in excess of 5,000 feet (1,600 meters).

The Shield, as with the rest of Quebec, was sculpted by ice sheets the size of Antarctica that advanced and retreated repeatedly over the past two million years. During the most prolonged cold spells these ice sheets were up to two miles thick. As they slowly moved south they chewed up and wore down the ancient rock of the Canadian Shield and stripped away the soil. When they gradually melted and retreated, they left behind displaced boulders ("erratics"), deep cuts ("striations") in the bedrock, mounds ("moraines") of dirt and rocks bulldozed by the glacier, and numerous lakes, bogs, rivers, and streams.

The dramatic effects of these ice sheets on the Canadian Shield section of Quebec have created both challenges and opportunities for inhabitants. The lack of deep soil and the unpredictable drainage patterns have hindered agriculture, though the short growing season is perhaps just as much a deterrent. The terrain does have small and isolated areas of arable land, though these are not sufficient to support large numbers of people. The more than one million rivers and lakes, however, attracted fur-bearing animals such as the beaver that provided an important natural resource for the First Nations (native tribes such as the Algonquin and Iroquois) as well as the earliest Europeans. More recently, the dramatic changes in elevation in the rivers as they plunge through falls and rapids have allowed for the development of an extensive hydroelectric (water-generating) power system. Finally, glaciation and other forces of erosion acting on the Shield have helped make mineral deposits more accessible. During the twentieth century, small communities have sprung up wherever mining operations have successfully extracted resources such as gold, silver, and nickel.

The Popular Uplands and Lowlands

The most southeastern section of Quebec, stretching some 500 miles (800 kilometers) from the so-called Eastern Townships area east of Montreal along the U.S. border and into the Gaspé Peninsula north of New Brunswick, harbors the Appalachian uplands region. (*Gaspé* is derived from the Native Mi'kmaqs' *Gespeg*, which means "the place where the land ends.") This uplands region is the northernmost end of the relatively old Appalachian mountain range estimated at 250 to 500 million years in age. Many of the peaks have been worn down by the effects of glaciation and erosion—the mountains on the southwestern end average only about 500 to 1,000 feet (150 to 300 meters)—but the peaks in the Gaspé Peninsula rise as high as 4,160 feet (1,268 meters).

On each side of the St. Lawrence River, in a wedge that widens from Quebec down to Montreal and finally to Quebec's border with New York State and southeast Ontario, lies the St. Lawrence lowlands. Even though Quebec is vast, four out of every five of Quebec's more than seven million people live on the St. Lawrence lowlands, whose 10,000 square miles (26,000 square kilometers) make up less than 2 percent of the province's total land area. Almost one in every two Quebecers lives in Montreal, while close to one in ten lives in Quebec City. Quebecers settled these areas, as did the First Nations before them, to use the St. Lawrence for transport and fishing. The surrounding area also offered soil that was sufficiently deep and rich, and the weather pleasant enough during the

■ *Montreal is the most populous metropolitan area in Quebec, with almost half of the province's inhabitants residing there.*

spring, summer, and fall for farming. Today the St. Lawrence lowlands remain Quebec's most fertile farmland, producing vegetables, grains, dairy products, and even fruits.

Even today, when modern technology can provide food and shelter in the harshest of climates, Quebecers have only barely spread out from the St. Lawrence lowlands. This continued concentration in the lowlands is partially the result of increases in the efficiency of agriculture, which have allowed more people to leave their farms and seek jobs in the cities. A century ago, 65 percent of Quebec's workforce lived in the countryside. Today only 20 percent do.

A Harsh Climate

While the rich farming land acted as a magnet attracting settlers to the lowlands, and the vast, inhospitable wilderness of the Canadian Shield crowding down on the lowlands from the north acted as a barrier discouraging settlers, another major factor determined the social development of Quebec: the climate. In general, once outside of the St. Lawrence lowlands, spring and fall are brief, and winter tends to be long and bitter as frigid polar air masses plummet the temperature to well below freezing for extended periods of time.

■ *Winters in Quebec are frigid; certain parts of the region receive snow for up to half the year.*

Because Quebec covers such a large area, however, the climate can differ considerably from one area to the next. For example, in the coastal areas of the Gaspé Peninsula, humid air brought in from over the Atlantic can yield clammy fogs and seemingly ceaseless rains. In the interior sections of the Appalachian uplands and St. Lawrence lowlands, the weather is more temperate, with summer days averaging in the high 70s° F (mid-20s° C). Even these parts of Quebec, however, experience real winter. Montreal may lie on the same latitude as the French Riviera, a well-known warm-weather resort, but it still averages some ten feet of snowfall a year, more than in Moscow or Oslo, Norway. Montreal can often have day after day of winter weather where the temperature hovers around—or below— 0° F (−18° C).

In the vast areas of central and northern Quebec, the winters are very harsh and continue for almost eight months. For

■ Adapting to Winter

Recognizing the beauty and bounteousness of the land, Quebecers have stayed, adapting to the harsh climate and even making a friend of winter. Of course, there are those snowbirds who go south during winter to places like Florida in order to avoid the winter altogether. And there are those who huddle inside. In cities like Montreal and Quebec, people can go right from their condos to an underground maze of stores, restaurants, hotels, theaters, and movie houses. In the suburbs, Quebecers make sure their houses are warm, using more energy to heat them than most other people in the world. And in an example of technology triumphing over nature, the newest high-tech farms use microprocessors to control the intensity of artificial lighting as well as heating, ventilation, and watering in greenhouses so farmers can grow crops during the dead of winter.

But for those hardy Quebec souls who love to get out even in the dead of winter, life is not really that harsh thanks to specially insulated coats, boots, and gloves that stave off the cold. For moving around, the snowshoes and sleds of the Indians worked well, but today's solutions are often more high-tech. Snow removal from the roads is so efficient—snowblowers made in Cap-Santé can handle two thousand tons of snow an hour—that roads are rarely blocked.

This efficiency, however, does come at a cost. In Ville de Quebec, a town of 168,000 people, it takes 250 men and women working all night to remove snow from the 400 miles of roadway and 300 miles of sidewalk in their area. In a one-year period, they applied over 12,000 tons of melting agents and abrasives and transported almost 50,000 truckloads of snow out of the town. Total cost for the year was over $21 million.

Only extremely heavy snowstorms ground flights for a few hours. Otherwise, even the most remote of Quebec's villages remain connected by air.

In the early years of settlement, ships could not move up the St. Lawrence River during winter because it would freeze over. In fact, the first European ships to arrive became stuck in the ice, to the great surprise and consternation of the sailors on board. Today, however, icebreakers keep the St. Lawrence Seaway open to ships all winter, all the way up to Montreal. Where roads are scarce, snowmobiles rule. Half the snowmobiles in the world are made in Quebec, moving people and things in snowbound locations.

■ *Young children in snowsuits brave the cold.*

summer, the inhabitants enjoy a short period of thawing and, on occasion, some very hot days (yet almost always cool nights). To illustrate the difference between the extremes, while all of Quebec experiences cold winters, it typically snows for only about three months of the year in the south, but for almost half the year in the north.

All this snow does not mean Quebec is a gray and miserable place to live, with skies always overcast. Even in December, when the days are shortest, the sun shines most days. In fact, the clear air and the sunlight reflecting off the snow make the land seem magical.

Not surprisingly, Quebecers have been quick to share their winter environment with tourists, skiing being an obvious attraction. One novel and increasingly popular sport is snowmobile-athons such as the annual Harricana International Snowmobile Race into the wilds of northcentral Quebec. These expeditions deep into the Shield allow tourists to marvel at the fantastic northern lights, or aurora borealis, and see herds of caribou.

Hardy Trees and Plants

While little of Quebec's flora can be appreciated during these winter expeditions, the province supports no fewer than four zones of vegetation, all established over the last three thousand years following the most recent ice age. The most northern region is tundra, and heading progressively south, one encounters the taiga with its boreal (northern) forest, mixed forest, and deciduous (hardwood) forest. The geology and climate of each area determine what vegetation they will support.

In the dry, rocky arctic and alpine areas that cover a quarter of the Canadian Shield, tundra (a Russian word for "flat-topped hill") dominates the landscape. This zone is almost totally lacking in tall trees or shrubs because the low year-round temperatures cause the soil, at a depth of a few feet, to be permanently frozen. With a growing season during the summer shorter than two months, the tundra appears barren but is hardly devoid of plant or animal life. In fact, if you look carefully, you can find some five hundred plant species, including low-lying shrubs, moss and lichens, and hearty grasses. This is enough to support a range of animals, from tiny rodents to the majestic caribou.

Between the tundra and the taiga (the rolling evergreen forest that extends all the way from Yukon Territory to southern Labrador) to the south is a transition zone, the forest-tundra, that can cover hundreds of miles. The rocky,

■ Quebec's First Botanists

During the bitterly cold winter of 1535–1536, ships under the command of the French explorer Jacques Cartier became stranded in twelve-foot-thick ice on the St. Lawrence River near the site of present-day Quebec City. The hundred or so French sailors soon came down with what Cartier termed "a pestilence . . . wholly unknown to us," according to Steven Leacock's account in *Canada: Foundations of Its Future.* Cartier noted that the sailors' "legs became swollen and puffed up. . . . Then the disease would creep up to the hips, thighs and shoulders, arm and neck. . . . The flesh peeled off down to the roots of their tooth, while the latter almost all fell out in turn."

For fear the Indians would slaughter them, the French hid their condition, and by the spring thaw, twenty-five men had died and all but three of the crew had the "pestilence." Modern medicine recognizes the ailment as scurvy, a condition that results from a lack of vitamin C. When the Indians found out, they immediately showed the French a cure—a tea brewed from the bark and leaves of the eastern white cedar, which is high in vitamin C.

The Indians continued to pass on their medical expertise to explorers, fur traders, and settlers over the following decades, including the use of red ochre for insect bites, balsam gum for wounds, and hemlock tea poultices for bruises and sprains. In all, native tribes made use of an estimated 275 species of plants for medicine, not to mention 130 species for food (including maple trees tapped for their sap) and 25 for dyes.

The first Frenchman to start investigating the medical possibilities of the area's plants was Michael Sarrazin, an army doctor who risked his life from Iroquois ambushes to identify native species between 1685 and his death in 1734. He discovered the carnivorous pitcher plant, which catches, drowns, and digests insects. He also recognized the potential of the Indian's maple syrup method and helped turn the manufacture of maple syrup into a major industry in Quebec, reducing the need to import sugar.

lichen-covered plateaus of the forest-tundra include scattered, mostly scrubby trees, numerous shallow lakes, and marshy bogs.

Another Russian word, *taiga* originally meant "a marshy forest in Siberia" but now refers to the thick boreal forest found south of the forest-tundra. In the taiga, winters are still fiercely cold and long, but the soil is not permanently frozen and it snows more. The boreal forest covers a quarter of Quebec and supports a variety of trees, especially conifers such as black spruce and balsam fir. As the climate becomes less severe, a wider range of life-forms is able to survive. Beneath the forest canopy you may find a carpet of moss, blueberry,

cloudberry, and other berry-bearing shrubs, and a range of ferns and small wildflowers. The boreal forests of Quebec's taiga also harbor some three hundred animal species, including the Canadian lynx, arctic fox, snowshoe hare, and American marten.

■ *A rocky, lichen-covered plateau in Quebec's tundra region.*

Further south, in the forests of the Laurentians, Appalachian uplands, and eastern lowlands, the boreal forest survives alongside deciduous forest. The combination of the two is a mixed forest zone that covers just over 10 percent of Quebec. Balsam fir and yellow and white birch predominate. This environment supports a wide range of habitats and diverse plants—more than a thousand plant species thrive, even in the cold temperatures—as well as 350 animal species, including large mammals such as moose and black bear.

Finally, in the very south of Quebec, and covering less than 7 percent of the province, is the deciduous forest zone. While the average temperature in the tundra zone is 18° F (−8° C), the average in the deciduous forest zone is 45° F (7° C), allowing it to support a far wider range of fauna and flora. Other significant factors in this diversity, which includes 1,600 plant species and almost 450 vertebrates, are fertile soils and close to 200 days of growing season.

Quebec's Abundant Animal Life

The abundant plant diversity, especially in southern Quebec, supports a wide variety of mammals, amphibians, and birds. Biologists have identified almost one hundred types of mammals in Quebec, including eight kinds of shrew, two of moles, eight types of bats, four of rabbits and hare, and no less than twenty-four rodent species, including porcupines, muskrats, lemmings, beavers, flying squirrels, chipmunks, and woodchucks. At the larger end of the scale lie deer, moose, and caribou. Among the carnivores at the top of the food chain are coyotes, gray wolves, foxes (gray, red, and arctic), mountain lions and bobcats, black and polar bears, raccoons, weasels, minks, and wolverines. Some of these mammals, like the skunk, were new to the earliest Europeans, one of whom observed in a report that the skunk "had a frightful smell, capable of making a whole canton [a district in Switzerland] a desert."[2] As for the mammals of the sea, whale watching is a popular pastime in eastern Quebec, where one can spy fourteen different whale species swimming off the coast, as well as six types of walrus and seal.

With all the lakes and rivers in the province, one would expect amphibians to thrive, and sure enough, frogs and salamanders are plentiful. These vertebrates, like all amphibians, possess smooth skin that allows water to evaporate easily, forcing them to live in and near water and to move about at night and during rains so as to avoid the danger of dehydrating. Their relatives the reptiles, on the other hand, which are represented in Quebec only by snakes and turtles, have a scaly skin that does not allow water to evaporate from their bodies and so enables them to survive away from water. Quebec supports more than three dozen species of both groups combined.

The wide wilderness is a haven largely undisturbed by human toxins for the 240 species of birds that either remain in Quebec or migrate there every summer. Quebec also has its own list of endangered species, including 13 fish, 23 mammals, and 22 bird species, among which are the golden and bald eagles, peregrine falcons, and the great gray owl.

While Quebec's countless lakes and rivers support a hundred species of freshwater fish, this number is relatively small compared, for instance, to the far smaller American state of

Ohio, which has over 170 fish species. The reason for the difference is that fish are still establishing themselves (and being introduced by humans) in Quebec, which a relatively short time ago (geologically) was under a sheet of ice and incapable of supporting fish populations. Ohio, on the other hand, was only partially glaciated.

■ *Whale watching is popular in the waters off eastern Quebec, where many whale species can be spotted.*

Lifeblood of the Land

A major factor in the biodiversity of the St. Lawrence lowlands is the St. Lawrence River, the 750-mile (1,200-kilometer) outlet that drains the five Great Lakes into the Atlantic Ocean. But the St. Lawrence is more than a simple river. For combined with the Great Lakes, the Ottawa, Saguenay, Saint Maurice, and Richelieu Rivers that feed into the St. Lawrence create one of the largest freshwater systems in the world. This entire watershed drains 40 percent of Quebec and in the process provides river, lake, and estuarine (an estuary is the area where a river empties into a sea) ecosystems that help support the diverse marine life in the area.

The rivers have been vital to humanity since the peoples of the First Nations navigated them in canoes and fished them for sustenance. The earliest Europeans also recognized the rivers as vital means of transport from the Atlantic into the Canadian interior, ever since the French first arrived and thought the St. Lawrence might be a route to the fabulous wealth of China. Indeed, French fur trappers known as

"voyageurs" traveled by canoe, with occasional portages (carrying the canoe over land), further and further along the rivers until they reached the northern and western reaches of Canada. For the majority who settled down to farm and trade, transport was also by canoe, with many farms designed to be long and thin so that each could have its own landing zone on a river. With the exception of military highways such as the one from Chamblis to Montreal, the early French colonists had little need to build roads.

Each year now, enormous grain and ore ships travel the St. Lawrence Seaway from the Atlantic to the western end of Lake Superior (a 4,600-mile, or 7,400-kilometer, round trip) carrying Canadian products to markets around the world. When parts of the Seaway—even saltwater sections—freeze over between December and April, a dozen icebreakers keep the lanes open to traffic.

Exporting Power

In addition to canals, another important water-related technology the Europeans introduced to Quebec when they arrived was the waterwheel—a harnessing of water for power. But rather than just powering one grain mill, for instance, the people of Quebec built dams to provide power for whole cities and even regions. Today, Hydro-Quebec's two-and-a-half-mile-long dam on the Eastmain River, which empties into James Bay (an extension of the Hudson Bay), holds back a reservoir of over 1,000 square miles (2,500 square kilometers) and powers one of the largest hydroelectric plants in the world. The thirty-seven generating stations provide electricity for almost half of Quebec.

■ Canals Make the Link

Because the St. Lawrence River is very young compared with most other rivers (perhaps only a few thousand years old in its current location), parts of it are somewhat difficult to navigate in parts. For example, rapids not far from Montreal can still pose a challenge to ships today. As the need arose for more reliable and navigable waterways, starting as early as the eighteenth century the French and then the British built canals to bypass falls and rapids and provide a deeper channel for large ships.

As economist Robin Neill has noted in "Francophone Quebec in the Canal Era," "The agricultural frontier in English-speaking Canada was a northern extension of the frontier expanding into the United States Midwest, and canals in Canada were built from New York through the Mohawk Gap in the Appalachians to Montreal, around Montreal Island, and up the St. Lawrence and the Ottawa Rivers, to penetrate the easternmost extension of the central plain." In addition to their importance to trade, these canals provided the British and French with an alternate route up and down the St. Lawrence River in case the Americans, located along the south bank, ever seized the whole waterway. Many historic canals still exist today and several, including Saint Ours, Chambly, and Carillon, are now the subject of federal legislation to preserve them.

The modern canals built during the twentieth century culminated with the opening of the St. Lawrence Seaway in 1959. For example, the 27-mile-long (44-kilometer-long) Welland Ship Canal, built in the early twentieth century to replace a one-hundred-year-old canal, links Lakes Erie and Ontario today and allows shipping to bypass Niagara Falls. Its eight locks can lift and lower ships and barges the more than 300-foot (100-meter) difference in altitude between the lakes. The Seaway thus provides large oceangoing ships access from the Atlantic all the way into the Great Lakes and the port cities of Toronto, Detroit, Chicago, and Buffalo.

■ *A ship enters the St. Lawrence Seaway.*

This remarkable engineering feat allowed Quebec to develop a natural resource—more flowing water than almost anywhere else on Earth—into a source of energy as well as jobs. The project also sparked fierce debate about its potential to harm the ecosystem (including beluga whales and caribou)

■ *Water from a Hydro-*
Quebec dam spillway
empties into James Bay.
This enormous dam
powers one of the world's
largest hydroelectric
plants.

as well as the traditional culture of the local First Nations groups. A proposed second stage of the project has been held up for decades by lawsuits filed by the Cree tribe.

The French, English, Cree, and other peoples who have made Quebec their home have confronted many challenges, in most cases learning to tame what they could and to shrug their shoulders and live with what they could not. From the days the first Asians claimed the land from the retreating glaciers, Quebecers have found ways to survive and thrive in harmony with nature.

The controversial James Bay projects show that while Quebecers can tame even the wildest of environments for potential economic gain, doing so may also reshape the social and political landscape. The many new waves of people who came to Quebec found plenty of challenges in the environment and in learning to live with one another. But the biggest challenge of all, to interact with one another and with the environment with long-term survival in mind, has still to be met.

The First Nations and European Pioneers

When the first European explorers arrived along the northeast coast of the New World in the early sixteenth century, they found a continent already inhabited by an estimated quarter of a million Native Amerindians. Some of these First Nations peoples had dwelled in the area of present-day Quebec for thousands of years. Many had formed complex societies with permanent dwellings and democratic political customs. As accomplished and powerful as these nations were, however, they were to find themselves facing desperate challenges in the coming years, not only from the newly arrived French and British but also from conflicts with one another.

So, too, did the earliest European pioneers need to adapt quickly to survive in a new and challenging environment. The cold climate, the limited prime farmland, and the sometimes unpredictable natives posed many hardships. The new pioneers quickly needed to learn how to persevere and become self-sufficient. The early conflicts and struggles that the First Nations and the French- and English-speaking people of Quebec endured have echoes in modern times that continue to influence provincial life.

A Land of Native Iroquois and Algonquins

In North America, the people of the First Nations established societies that varied widely depending upon local conditions. By 1500 the area of present-day Quebec province harbored at

least a dozen distinct tribes, ranging from the Inuit (Eskimo) of the far north to the Mi'kmaq of the Gaspé Peninsula. Certainly, two of the First Nations peoples that would play the greatest role in the future of the area were the Iroquois and the Algonquins (also known as Algonkin).

Sometime in the fifteenth century, five First Nations peoples, (Mohawk, Oneida, Onondaga, Cayuga, and Seneca) centered around current upstate New York and the lower St.

■ *A seventeenth-century engraving by a French explorer depicts Iroquois Indians building a boat. The Iroquois played an important role in the history of Quebec.*

Lawrence River valley, banded together to form a league or confederacy known as the Iroquois. These five tribes, later to be joined by a sixth nation (the Tuscarora), referred to themselves as "the people of the longhouse." Literally, the clans (multifamily groupings typically controlled by a matron) inhabited distinctive wooden structures, and symbolically each tribe lived within a giant longhouse. Thus, for example, the Mohawk, centered around present-day Albany, were "keepers of the eastern door."

The Iroquois were both hunters and growers. The men of the Iroquois tribes stalked deer and other game while the women were the principal growers and cooks. Garden plots created by cutting or burning the forest were planted with maize (Indian corn), squash, sunflowers, and various beans. Women pounded the dried corn in a wooden mortar to make flour and pressed the sunflower seeds to make oil. Depending upon the tribe, some women also helped catch fish or birds, find eggs, and gather roots and berries. Any surplus they dried and stored for the winter when game might be scarce. By supplementing hunting with agricultural products, they were able to avoid the feast and famine that plagued those societies that only hunted.

In contrast to the Iroquois tribes, the Algonquins circa 1500 were a seminomadic hunting and trapping people. Their main location was more northerly than the Iroquois, especially along the Ottawa River, where the growing season was too short and the climate too cool for extensive farming. Thus the Algonquins did not build the wooden houses and fortified villages in the fashion of their Iroquois neighbors, but found it more useful to construct conical-shaped tipis or

■ Cartier's View of the Longhouses

Here is how the pioneering French explorer Jacques Cartier described the distinctive wooden buildings of the Iroquois in a journal entry, as quoted in Steven Leacock's *Canada: Foundations of Its Future*:

> The village is circular and is completely enclosed by a wooden palisade in three tiers, like a pyramid. The top one is built crosswise, the middle one perpendicular, and the lowest one of strips of wood placed length-wise. The whole is well joined and lashed after their manner, and is some two lances in height. There is only one gate and entrance to this village, and that can be barred up. Over this gate, and in many places above the enclosure, are species of galleries with ladders for mounting to them, which galleries are provided with rocks and stones for the defense and protection of the place. There are some 50 houses in this village, each about 50 or more paces in length and 12 or 15 in width, built completely of wood and covered in and boarded up with large pieces of bark and rind of trees, as broad as a table, which are well and cunningly lashed after their manner. And inside these houses are many rooms and chambers; and in the middle is a large space without a floor, where they light their fire and live together in common. Afterwards, the men retire to the above-mentioned quarters with their wives and children. And furthermore, there are lofts in the upper part of their houses, where they store the corn, of which they make their bread.

■ *An Iroquois man outside a reconstructed Iroquois longhouse.*

dome-shaped wigwams covered with birch bark. The Algonquins were skilled woodspeople, capable of using seemingly primitive tools such as stone axes to build huge canoes that helped the Algonquin men become well-traveled traders.

The Lure of China Attracts Explorers

These First Nations peoples were completely unknown to the Europeans when explorers began to arrive at the end of the fifteenth century. John Cabot, an Italian-born explorer who made two voyages for the British King Henry VII in the late

■ *An illustration shows Italian explorer John Cabot's first landing in North America.*

1490s, was the first European since the Vikings five hundred years earlier to reach the coast of North America. Instead of the rich lands of the Orient that he had hoped to encounter, however, he found mostly barren rock at his landing on what is now believed to be either Newfoundland or Cape Breton Island. His trips were not wasted, however. He reported sailing through untold numbers of fish near what is now known as the Grand Banks, off the east coast of Newfoundland. His tales, and the experiences of other intrepid fishing expeditions, soon inspired growing numbers of English, French, and Portuguese to explore the mysterious northern shores of the New World.

In 1534 one of these sailors, the French explorer Jacques Cartier, explored the broad gulf of the Atlantic guarded by present-day Newfoundland and Nova Scotia. Landing on the Gaspé Peninsula, he claimed the land for the French king Francis I. Like others of the time, Cartier was hoping to find a route to the Orient and its supply of gold, spices, and fabulous riches. His hopes probably soared when he spied the mouth of a huge river, 90 miles (145 kilometers) wide at its mouth, that empties into the gulf. Cartier named the river after a Christian martyr, Saint Laurent, whose feast day coincided with the day of Cartier's discovery.

Cartier had to sail back to France without exploring this potential route to China, but he did initiate a lasting French interest in the New World. The following year he returned and explored south down the wide inlet of the St. Lawrence. When the river narrowed to less than one mile (two kilometers) Cartier spied a large native village on a promontory on the northern shore. Upon coming ashore he learned that the native Iroquois called it Stadacona. This settlement was later to become the site of the city of Quebec. (*Quebec* is thought to be derived from an Algonquian word meaning "narrowing of the river.")

Cartier left a number of men to winter at this village and continued upstream to another prominent village, Hochelaga. Cartier climbed a hill near the village and dubbed it Mount Royal—"Mont Réal." His thoughts of China were encouraged by Indian reports that the river went on a great distance to the west. To Cartier's disappointment, the rapids north of Montreal, which he wistfully named "Lachine" (China), blocked the progress of large ships.

■ *French explorer Jacques Cartier claims the Gaspé Peninsula for the French king in 1534.*

■ *Samuel de Champlain and his crew explore the Canadian wilderness with the aid of friendly local Indians.*

Champlain's First Settlement

Neither the French nor any other European power managed to settle the area visited by Cartier for the remainder of the sixteenth century. It was the French explorer Samuel de Champlain who in 1608 established the first permanent French settlement, at Quebec City. He was helped by friendly Algonquin Indians who taught the French how to survive in the harsh climate and acted as guides to the new terrain.

Champlain and the French settlers had arrived in the midst of a long-simmering war between Iroquois and Algonquin tribes. Champlain was slow to realize, however, that by befriending the Algonquins the French were in danger of making lasting enemies of the Iroquois. One incident in particular was to have a long-term effect on French and Indian affairs. In the summer of 1609, Champlain and a dozen other Frenchmen were exploring west of Quebec City when they came upon a large group of Algonquins and Huron preparing to travel south to invade the homeland of the Mohawk, one of the Iroquois tribes. Champlain and two Frenchmen accompanied the war party all the way to a large lake (which Champlain named for himself) some 50 miles (80 kilometers) south of Montreal.

Mohawk warriors gathered on the shore of the lake to defend their land, but the battle was over quickly due to the French guns. As Champlain noted, "When I saw them make a move to draw their bows upon us, I took aim with my Aquebus, and shot straight at one of the three chiefs. And with this shot, two fell to the ground and one of their companions was wounded. This frightened the enemy greatly."[3] The battle was the Indians' first exposure to firearms in battle. Over the next few years the Algonquins used their access to French guns to gain an advantage over the Iroquois. The Iroquois, however, were quick to make allies of the Dutch and the British and to equip themselves with firearms, too. The Iroquois soon regarded the French as deadly enemies.

The French and Algonquins, on the other hand, got along well. Champlain treated the Algonquins as equals and they respected him. "Our sons shall wed your daughters," he told

■ *Champlain and his party, with the help of the Algonquins, defeat a group of Mohawk warriors in 1609.*

them, "and henceforth we shall be one people." When Champlain died in the winter of 1635, hundreds of local Indians attended his funeral. The Huron came in the next summer with presents to help the French "wipe away their tears."[4]

The Beaver Economy

If the search for the riches of the East brought the Europeans to Quebec, it was furs that prompted them to stay. Beavers not only numbered in the millions but they were also very easy to catch. By the late seventeenth century, one hundred thousand beaver pelts were being shipped annually from New France. Many French traders were making huge profits. Predictably, beavers were soon growing scarce in the wilderness surrounding the St. Lawrence River valley, and trappers and traders had to push west for fresh supplies.

The French regarded their alliance with the Algonquins as crucial for the fast-developing fur trade. Champlain had explored as far west as Lake Huron in search of the route to China, and although he didn't find it, he did establish a canoe-borne fur trade that set the stage for further colonization. The Algonquins and other First Nations people were eager to barter furs for European firearms and other goods. High-grade North American furs were much valued in Europe for their warmth. There was also a steady demand for the short, dense undercoats of the beaver, which were the best material for making felt cloth and the large felt hats like the "copatain" that were then fashionable.

The Runners in the Woods

While the French were happy at first for the local Indians to bring them pelts, after a while the French "coureurs de bois," or runners in the woods, ventured further and further into the wilderness. Often these runners were young men who decided that rather than tilling the fields under the watchful eye of parents or the church pastor, they would rather be out in the wilds wearing buckskins, looking for furs, and getting rich. Growing numbers of these young men became coureurs de bois who would meet directly with the Indians and encourage them to trap more beavers. As the runners pushed west, they set up trading and staging posts that provided links back to Quebec City and Montreal.

At their peak, the coureurs de bois numbered only about six hundred, but their influence was far-reaching. They had increased trade and contact between the French and the

■ Explorer Etienne Brule

Etienne Brule was a bright and adventurous sixteen-year-old in 1608 when he accompanied Champlain as his servant on the voyage from France to the site of the new settlement of Quebec. Only two years later, Brule obtained permission from Champlain to live among the local Huron Indians. In June 1611, Brule returned to Quebec dressed in skins and speaking fluent Algonquian. Champlain appointed Brule his representative in the wilderness, allowing him to explore widely and eventually to become (thanks in large part to Indian guidance) the first European to see four of the Great Lakes (Huron, Michigan, Superior, and Ontario). Brule is considered the first true coureur de bois, with his explorations taking him as far south as present-day Pennsylvania and Maryland.

During one adventure, when a war party of Iroquois captured Brule, it looked as if he would be tortured and killed. But one of the warriors grabbed a religious pendant from Brule's neck just as lightning lit up the sky and thunder boomed across the Indian's campsite. Brule told the Iroquois it was God speaking, and they let him go.

He was not quite so lucky later in his life, when he switched sides and began to work for the British in 1629. Brule helped the British capture Quebec, in what would be the first of many struggles between the French and British for control of the city. Champlain returned to Quebec four years later (a 1632 treaty had returned Quebec to the French) to find that the Huron had apparently murdered Brule, perhaps because he had betrayed their friend, Champlain.

Indians and explored much of central Canada. In other respects their actions were cause for concern. Indian authorities, for example, began to recognize the potential harm from the alcohol the coureurs de bois often sold to Indians. Civil and religious authorities in New France also began to consider the coureurs de bois a harmful influence, tempting young men of the colony into the woods and away from more useful roles as farmers and soldiers. This led to attempts to outlaw the coureurs de bois in 1680, and ultimately their declining role in frontier society.

Farming Emerges to Rival Fur Trading

Many of the French who came to settle the New World were no more interested in trading fur than they were in fighting the Iroquois. They wanted only land of their own to farm. In addition to the hardships presented by freezing winters and unfriendly natives, right from the start they also had to deal with fur traders who resented the farmers as competition. With some justification, the fur traders believed that farming would destroy the cover for the wild animals and make it harder to find and trade in furs.

These fur traders had initially directed their anger at Louis Herbert, the first French farmer to bring French crops and tools to Quebec and establish a farm. It took him a year to clear an area of forest, and in 1618 he planted ten acres of wheat, corn, peas, beans, and even apple trees outside Quebec City, using an axe, a pick, and a spade. By the time he died in 1626, Herbert was able to support his family with his own produce. Two years later, the first ox team and plow arrived, making farming much easier for his successors.

Tradesmen and farmers helped each other to clear land and build houses. Some of these early houses were built with four-feet-thick stone walls because, being held together only with lime mortar, they would fall apart if made any thinner. But the thickness also helped cool the occupants during the summer and keep them warm in winter. The men also built steep roofs so the snow would slide off during winter before the weight of the snow collapsed the roof. The interior designs were simple, with one large room downstairs and bedrooms upstairs.

New France Slow to Grow

The rift between traders and farmers was only one reason why life for European settlers was difficult and dangerous during the early days of New France. The constant skirmishing between the French and Iroquois has led some to refer to the entire period of 1630 to 1700 as the "Beaver Wars." Battles and raids caused the death of fifty to one hundred colonists, and probably more natives, during the 1650s. In 1658 the Iroquois even launched an all-out offensive against Montreal that almost succeeded in capturing it. Fur trading and even farming became so dangerous that many colonists returned to France because they were unable to work their fields without fear of attack. As a result, the French population grew very slowly.

The slow development of New France troubled France's King Louis XIV, who reigned from 1661 to 1715. Although the lands in the New World claimed by the French were at least a three-week sail from France and were as yet peopled only with a handful of adventurers and peasants, they offered tremendous opportunity for wealth through the fur trade. Louis recognized that if French land claims in the New World

■ Frontier Justice

In the absence of a strong government and an established police force, the law and its enforcement on the frontier tended to be rather uneven, if not barbaric, and New France was no exception. If a man would not stop swearing, his lips would be burned with a hot poker. Often, death was the penalty for robbery, rape, and arson, and it certainly was for murder, with the guilty generally being tortured before being put to death.

In much of New France laws aimed at women were particularly restrictive. Women had to be home by nine, and unmarried girls were permitted to dance only with each other in their homes under the watchful eye of their mothers. Rouge was forbidden. When one man had an affair with a married woman, he was banished from the town and fined 600 livres, but the husband of the woman was given the option of keeping her in jail for the rest of her life or returning her to her father and mother. Luckily for this married woman, he did neither and they reconciled to raise a large family.

In some parts of early New France, however, more-benign rules prevailed. For example, in Ville Marie, which had been founded as a religious community on Montreal Island, if anyone was caught fighting, they had to pay the victim's medical bills. If one person insulted another, they had to admit publicly that the other was indeed respectable. When one man tried to rape a married woman, over three acres of his land was taken and given to the woman's children and the Church.

could be extended, France could better compete with other European powers in the race to create new colonies and expand trade.

In 1663 Louis decided to take over the running of the colony from the church and trading bodies that had managed it for the previous 150 years. Louis immediately identified two key problems. One was the constant harassment from the Iroquois. Louis sent heavily armed French troops and by 1667 the Iroquois had been forced to accept a lasting truce. The second problem would take longer to address: France had only 3,215 people in the whole of New France (according to the first official census taken in 1666) compared to one hundred thousand British subjects in the American colonies along the Eastern Seaboard.

Go Forth and Multiply

As it was proving hard to persuade Frenchmen to emigrate to the new colony, Louis ordered that women be sent instead— young girls who could marry the men still in New France and bear many children. Eleven hundred French peasant girls arrived in New France, and even though only ten thousand French people emigrated to New France over the next century, these "King's Daughters" as they were known succeeded in raising the numbers of French in Quebec to sixty-five thousand by the mid-1700s. Two centuries later, those numbers had increased to more than 5 million.

Louis went further in his program to populate New France. Fathers were fined if they did not ensure their sons were married by eighteen years of age and their daughters by age fifteen. Until their offspring were all married, the fathers then had to report in every six months to explain why the young people were still single. For those parents who raised ten or more children, on the other hand, the king provided a

■ *In an effort to populate New France, King Louis XIV sent eleven hundred French peasant girls to the colony to marry men already living there.*

pension of 300 livres a year. If the parents had twelve children, the reward rose to 400 livres. Of course, the drawback was that the father then had to make sure all those children married on time to avoid being fined.

Bachelors in New France who failed or refused to marry also faced problems. Jean Tallon, the first supervisor of New France, denied them rights to hunt, fish, or trade with the Indians. The minister in France responsible for developing New France ordered that "those who may seem to have absolutely renounced marriage should be made to bear additional burdens, and be excluded from all honors; it would be well even to add some marks of infamy."[5]

François Le Noir of Lachine was taken to court for trading with the Indians while a bachelor. He was allowed to continue trading as long as he promised to marry a lady from the next boatload of girls, or he would be fined 300 livres. He kept his promise. The pressure to marry was so great that one woman whose first husband died in Montreal in 1672 was married to another man before the first was even buried. As strange as these measures may seem today, they were effective in increasing the population of New France.

■ The King's Daughters

When Louis XIV ordered girls be sent to New France to marry, the first girls chosen were taken from the orphanages in Paris. But these girls were not strong enough to survive the endless hard work and rough conditions. Plan B called for strong and healthy country girls, "free from any natural blemish or anything personally repulsive." The local priest was required to give each a certificate showing that she was not married and of good moral character.

The girls were given free passage to New France and met by bachelors as they disembarked. These men inspected the girls "just as a butcher does a ewe from amongst a flock of sheep." The fattest girls were the most prized, because they were the most likely to survive the cold winters. The men were expected to declare what possessions they had and how they made their living. The girls were most interested in men who owned a farm.

The girls could reject an offer of marriage, but they were not too fussy, as they had little future ahead of them without a husband. A girl could leave her husband only if he beat her with a stick that was thicker than his wrist. Some marriages were performed right on the quay and the girls given a dowry on behalf of the king, which may have included land, tools, household items, animals, barrels of salted meat, and even a small amount of money.

■ *Native Americans swap their furs for rifles. Trade, and an increasing reliance on French goods, allowed the Europeans to gain control over the region's native inhabitants.*

First Nations in Decline

The steady growth of New France over the sixteenth and seventeenth centuries coincided with a slow decline in the First Nations. Their traditional way of life was fast disappearing as they increasingly adopted a version of the white man's lifestyle. As Chief Dan George (1899–1981) was to observe later, "When the white man came, we had the land and they had the bibles. Now they have the land and we have the bibles."[6]

In many respects, when the French first arrived in the New World their culture was inferior to that of the local First Nations. The French, after all, had to rely on the native peoples for assistance just to survive. And sixteenth-century French peasants did not really live in better conditions than those prevailing in the longhouses of the Iroquois. Nor was European medicine at the time superior.

The Indians had helped the Europeans survive and prosper, and what the natives received in return was the products of industry but not the industry itself—iron pots and steel weapons but not the means to produce such items. Native culture was also being forced to adapt to whiskey and firearms as well as to deadly new diseases such as smallpox that Native Amerindians lacked exposure to (and thus had less immunity against compared to Europeans).

The triple threat of what one cultural historian has dubbed "guns, germs, and steel" allowed the French to insert themselves into the region permanently and to gain increasing control over the land and the lives of its former inhabitants. The days of intense colonization were beginning, as European powers jockeyed to gain control and wealth of vast lands across the world. The Iroquois and Algonquins were about to become pawns, and Quebec a few squares on the gameboard, of this power struggle.

The French and British Struggle for Power

Although in recent centuries the French and British have been allies rather than enemies in war, the early struggles between the two major European cultures of Quebec have never been resolved completely. Conflicts between French- and English-speaking peoples in Quebec continue to surface even today in wars of words—literally in this case, since disputes have raged over issues such as whether signs should be in French only or bilingual. The battles in earlier centuries, however, involved a good deal more bloodshed.

A Fifty-Year War

Not content with having their colonies only in New England, the British had established a settlement in Newfoundland in 1610 and in Nova Scotia in 1629. They then expanded into Quebec with the creation of the Hudson's Bay Company in 1670, competing directly against the French in the fur trade. When war broke out between France and Britain in 1689, it spread naturally to their colonies.

A British fleet of thirty ships sailed for Quebec. A few hundred French soldiers, "habitants" (French who had emigrated to and were living in Quebec), and priests fired upon and held off the British forces of two thousand men. In the northern reaches of James Bay, the French and the English fought several times over Fort Albany in Ontario and Fort Rupert in Quebec. Twice the English were defeated and twice the French driven off. Finally, in the early eighteenth century, the French gained the upper hand.

Calm Before Another Storm

France's renewed control over New France was to last only until 1730. Because the British had beaten the French in the battlefields of Europe, France's King Louis XV, by signing the Treaty of Utrecht, ceded most of the maritime states, as well as Hudson Bay, to the British. As most of the French in New France lived in southern Quebec, not in the areas given to the British, the treaty still allowed the French to govern themselves and most of New France.

Despite this loss, especially of the fur trade in the Hudson Bay hunting grounds, the French in New France were finally able to build and grow without their efforts being thwarted by war and Indian raids. The economy flourished. Shipyards were built and tar factories and sawmills began to operate along the St. Lawrence. In 1738, the first forge was put into operation near Trois-Rivières, producing stoves, pots, plowshares, tools, and anchors—items that no longer had to be shipped from France. Crop production tripled between 1721 and 1739.

By 1734 the first road in Quebec, Le Chemin du Roi, connected Montreal and Quebec. Immigrants began to flood into New France; combined with the high birth rate, French men and women in New France numbered seventy-four thousand by 1755. The standard of living rose above the roughness of frontier life to the point where it was now a match for the fineries of France.

All was still not well, however. Even though the British were presumably at peace with the French in the New World, tensions between the two countries remained high back on the European continent. The British attacked French shipping—three hundred ships in 1755 alone—creating shortages in New France. The following year, Britain and France were again embroiled in conflict as they engaged in what came to be known as the Seven Years' War.

Britain Conquers New France

While New France had less than seven thousand troops, the British had increased their troop strength in North America to twenty-three thousand. When the British attacked, the French hoped their King would send reinforcements and ships, but he told them he had none to spare. The French situation became

desperate in New France: With most men fighting the British, few could till the fields to feed the colony, and the British were still capturing most of the French supply ships.

 *Well-dressed French settlers stroll along a dock. As Quebec's population increased, so did its standard of living.*

By 1759 the British had captured all the French forts outside of Quebec City. They then arrived off Quebec in June with 168 ships and 22,000 sailors and soldiers. Facing them were 16,000 Frenchmen aged from twelve to eighty. The British managed to reach the walled city, but instead of waiting behind the wall for the British ships to become iced in by the approaching winter, the French General Louis Montcalm ordered his men to battle in a field adjoining the city. Under General James Wolfe, the English troops won this decisive Plains of Abraham battle on September 13, 1759. The French retreated behind the walls of the city but were soon forced to surrender. The subsequent surrender of Montreal to the British in 1760 effectively put an end to New France as a French colony.

The signing of the Treaty of Paris in 1763 formally transferred power over New France to the British. Unwilling to accept British rule, many of the middle-class French families returned to France. They left behind sixty-five thousand farmers, trappers, missionaries, and others. Many of these early French Canadians were no doubt troubled by the prospect of a new life under British rule, but they banded even closer together to preserve their unique customs and identity.

■ *An illustration depicts the 1759 Plains of Abraham battle. The British victory in this battle resulted in their gaining control of New France.*

British Rule by Compromise

The few British now in control of the area were faced with the task of governing tens of thousands of Frenchmen, their longtime rivals for power and wealth from across the Channel. The French spoke their own language (though the British ruling class was also fluent in French), had their own criminal and civil legal systems, and embraced a religion (Roman Catholicism) that the notorious English king Henry VIII had famously rejected more than two centuries earlier, leading the way to widespread British Protestantism. Conflict seemed inevitable, but the British made some astute moves.

A Royal Proclamation in 1763 arranged for Quebec to have a governor general and an elected assembly. When British merchants from Boston arrived in Quebec and tried to dominate the assembly, Guy Carleton, the French-speaking British commander who had become governor in 1768, would not bend to their pressure and insisted upon an elected assembly. Roman Catholic worship was to be tolerated, although Catholics were not permitted to hold public office nor to sit on juries. On the other hand, English law was to be used, a decision that rankled the French.

The British made further concessions to the overwhelmingly French-speaking citizens when Parliament passed the Quebec Act of 1774. This gave Catholics full political rights and religious freedom. The Roman Catholic Church was once again allowed to collect tithes (taxes representing one-tenth of total income) from its parishioners. French civil law was reinstituted, although criminal law remained British. Whether these British efforts to accommodate their French colony were enough to establish a bond of allegiance was shortly to face a strong test in the form of the American Revolutionary War.

■ Montreal's Annual Fur-Trading Fair

At the close of the eighteenth century, Montreal played host each year to a gala fur-trading fair. Hundreds of Indians, some of whom had paddled their canoes thousands of miles, would bring up to one hundred thousand pelts to trade. The fair began with the smoking of the "calumet," the pipe of peace, and the singing of the peace song. Then the barter would begin. The Indians were very specific about what they desired in return for their goods. At the top of their list were muskets, powder, and shot or musket balls, all of which they had come to depend upon for hunting. They also wanted other useful European manufactured items, such as metal kettles, woolen blankets, and linen cloth. The woven materials may not have been as warm as the animal skins the Indians were accustomed to, but when textiles became wet, they dried much faster than furs.

Other items, often more popular with the men than the women, were jewelry and body paints, vermilion being their favorite color. Looking glasses (mirrors) were also a sought-after item. According to Edgar Collard's account in *Montreal: The Days That Are No More*, an English visitor, John Palmer, reported, "The Indians were dressed in all their finery; blue leggings, trimmed with scarlet list, a gay printed shirt, a black or common blanket thrown over their shoulders, and a gaudy yarn sash round their waist; some had their faces painted red and black, etcetera; some had plates of silver on . . . and almost all had pendulous earrings."

Unfortunately, brandy and rum were also in great demand, and the French provided it, despite the misgivings of their church, because the Indians would trade with the British or Dutch, who would provide the alcohol if the French did not. As Collard goes on to say, another English traveler who visited the Montreal fair in September 1768 noted, "They have their rum in a keg, the bung of which they set to their mouth, drinking round and never quitting it 'til the vessel is quite emptied. This brings on a temporary madness; and, so long as it continues, they're guilty of the most enormous excesses."

An American General Wins Few Friends

When the Americans invaded the British colony of Quebec during the American war of independence, most Frenchmen did not care to become involved in the conflict. Some sympathized with the American cause, as did most of the people of France—the French government ultimately lent important wartime support to the American rebels. Other residents of Quebec, particularly the clergy and landowners, wanted to stay with the British, whom they saw as more likely than the Americans to respect Catholicism and French customs. Many Quebecois reasoned that their ability to maintain their identity and culture would be easier as a remote British colony than as a minority society in a continental republic.

By fall 1775 the Americans were in a strong position, having captured Montreal and a number of smaller British-controlled cities in Quebec. They needed only to treat the French well and capture Quebec City, defended by a few French militia and English troops, to drive the British out of Canada. To counter the expected American attack on Quebec City, Carleton had eighteen hundred men at his disposal, more than half of them French volunteers. He ordered any American sympathizers to leave Quebec City and, surprisingly, most of the English merchants left. These were strange alliances indeed.

But the Americans made a major mistake during the winter of 1775: They sent Brigadier General David Wooster to command the American occupation troops in Montreal. Wooster's heavy-handed approach quickly angered the people of Montreal. On one occasion, he threatened to exile top-ranking officials and clergy to the American colonies. On Christmas Eve, he closed all the Roman Catholic churches to prevent the traditional celebration of midnight mass. He sent forty sleds crowded with "Tory conspirators" to Albany in the freezing winter weather because they were guilty of "ungenerous conduct." When some

■ *Brigadier General David Wooster commanded the American occupation troops in Montreal.*

citizens approached Wooster to protest his actions, he told them, "I regard the whole lot of you as enemies and rascals."[7] When a judge then complained in writing, Wooster locked him up for five weeks before deporting him to Albany. Wooster then ordered notices be nailed to all church doors forbidding anyone to talk about American affairs.

The last straw for New French patience with their American "guests" came when Wooster wrote to the Continental Congress that "there is but little confidence to be placed in the Canadians; they are but a small remove from the savages."[8] The British obtained a copy of the letter and made sure it found its way into the hands of the clergy in Montreal, who told all their parishioners how their American "liberators" really felt about the French people of Quebec.

When word reached the Continental Congress of this budding public relations disaster in Montreal, they sent a party including Benjamin Franklin to Montreal to influence the Canadian people. The Franklin party's arrival in April 1776, however, was too late. By then the American siege of Quebec City, which had begun on December 31, 1775, had started to falter. British reinforcements in the spring of 1776 forced the undersupplied Americans to retreat from Quebec City. The British then routed the Americans in a series of smaller skirmishes over the next three months, and by July the Americans had fled south in retreat. As the Americans were retreating from Montreal, Benedict Arnold ordered the city burned, but the French citizens extinguished the flames. This final act by the American forces reinforced what had become apparent during the fighting: Whatever differences the French and British in Quebec may have had, they were now allied against a new, common, and stronger foe south of the St. Lawrence River.

Quebec Gets Cut in Half

The American revolutionaries enjoyed greater success in America. When they won their independence, many British subjects in the American colonies, as well as their Iroquois allies, fled into the southern and western parts of Quebec. To avoid any potential conflict between the Protestant British and the Catholic French, the British parliament passed the Constitutional Act in 1791, splitting Quebec into Upper Canada (the future Ontario), where most of the recently arrived British had fled, and Lower Canada (the future Quebec), where the French had been settled for years. The French-speaking province was therefore given its own legislative assembly, and the many British subjects who had fled the United States were able to govern themselves, too. It looked as if the British government and the French and British peoples in Canada had come together and formed a workable framework for coexistence, but mismanagement by the British was to jeopardize this arrangement.

For the next three decades, Lower Canada prospered and its population increased dramatically as a result of one of the highest birth rates in the world. When the demand for fur and the fur trade finally collapsed in the 1820s, most Quebecois turned to farming, fishing, or boatbuilding for their livelihoods. Many also entered the church to become clergy or missionaries. In contrast, the British, though a minority, still held enough of the reins of power to dominate in the fields of business and politics. Most of the people of the province who were lawyers, merchants, and bankers were British, not French. This disparity would haunt the province for the next two centuries.

Britain's political dominance came about because the provincial governor, appointed by the British parliament, in turn appointed the Executive and Legislative Councils. These small groups of men could overrule the provincial Assembly, even though that body was elected by the French majority. The governor also decided how money raised by taxes was to be spent and how much money government officials were to be paid. In the early 1800s, governors in both Lower and Upper Canada appointed Tory (fiercely loyal British) friends to the Councils. Englishmen were appointed to the top positions in the government and legal system. Economic and political life was soon dominated by a small, unelected group of wealthy Englishmen.

Then in 1822, a bill was proposed by the British House of Commons to unite Upper and Lower Canada. If this were to pass, the French would become a minority in their own land. This threat, combined with the way the Tories in Canada were running the government for their own ends at the expense of the French, gave birth to a French nationalism committed to defending French interests in Canada. The clergy, who had initially supported the British, were now at the center of the demand for French Canadian sovereignty within the greater Canadian colony. Initial attempts by the French to find a solution through legislation turned into violence with the insurrection of 1837 and the so-called Patriot War during the following two years.

The Insurrection of 1837

For many years, Louis Papineau, the speaker in the Lower Canada Legislative Assembly and the leader of the Reform

Party, campaigned for an elected and representative government. Although violence occurred during an election in 1832 and British troops fired into the crowd, killing three French Canadians, the patriot movement was generally a peaceful one.

In 1834, Les Patriotes was a growing group of French Canadians who wanted representative government for the French-speaking majority. They presented 92 resolutions to the Assembly, demanding, among other things, representative government and impeachment of the governor. The Assembly adopted the resolutions, and the 23 men who voted against them were defeated in the next general election. Three years later, when the British government ignored the 92 resolutions and presented ten of their own, Les Patriotes resorted to violence. The governor issued warrants for the arrest of 26 Patriote leaders, and it took 600 British troops to restore order, as Patriote leaders were caught and then freed again by other Patriotes.

The 1837 insurrection was short-lived, but because French concerns were not addressed, they reappeared the next year in fighting known as the Patriot War. Meanwhile the insurrection did have some effect on the British, who did not want to lose their Canadian colony on the heels of the loss of the American colonies.

The Patriot War

The British had arrested 500 Patriotes following the 1837 insurrection, and released 200 of them in January 1838. In May the British released a hundred more Patriotes, and when Lord Durham arrived to conduct his enquiry that month, he declared a general amnesty that allowed all but eight of the remaining 200 Patriotes still in prison to go free. Those eight were exiled to Bermuda.

In addition to raids by exiled Canadians and idealistic Americans from the United States, resistance to British rule continued from the Canadian arm of a secret society called Les Frères Chasseurs (the Hunter Brethren) in Montreal. Their emblem showed a rifle crossed with a dagger because, if they were caught with firearms, they would tell the British they were out hunting. Their numbers increased to fifty thousand, but because they were never led effectively or armed sufficiently well, they accomplished little.

In November they skirmished with British troops, and by December over 800 were in prison, with 12 of the 99 condemned to death actually being executed. In the same month, 400 men left New York for Canada, half of them deserting

■ *A painting depicts a skirmish between British troops and rebels during the 1837 Patriot War.*

before they arrived, including the commander. They took shelter in a windmill and surrendered after five days and the loss of seventeen American and sixteen Canadian lives.

Militarily the Patriot War was a shambles for the French Canadians, accomplishing little at the cost of a few lives and the burning of a few buildings. While the British Canadians were fairly restrained in dealing with the war and its perpetrators, they showed less understanding of the concerns that prompted the war in the first place.

From Colony to Province

Lord Durham was sent from Britain in 1837 to investigate the causes of the uprisings in both Upper and Lower Canada. "I found two nations warring within the bosom of a single state: I found a struggle, not of principles, but of races,"[9] he famously commented. To satisfy the English community, he recommended that Upper and Lower Canada be reunited. To please the French, he recommended that the Councils be made up of elected officials from the majority party. Unfortunately the British government felt that a government responsible to the people would be too independent, and so it authorized only the reunion of Upper and Lower Canada, which took effect in 1841.

The French were not pleased with this development. Nor were they happy with Durham's other recommendations: that the French population be assimilated into the British majority and that French no longer be considered an official language. By this time, however, the French had limited power to influence events and could do little more. As events later showed, French nationalism was not dead—merely asleep.

By 1848, Canada was given greater freedom from Britain when it was granted the right to govern itself in all matters except foreign affairs. For the Quebecois, this meant little when the real power lay in the hands of English Quebecers.

In 1860 something happened to improve the poor relations between the British of Ontario and the French of Quebec: Once again, their common enemy—the Americans to the south of the border—threatened. This time, the fact that the Canadians were maintaining trading relations with the Confederacy angered the Union forces during the American Civil War. They called for an invasion of Canada, a threat that was real, given the immense size of the Union army.

Although Union troops never carried out this threat, it was enough to bring the British together with English- and French-speaking Canadians to defend what was an increasingly real Canadian identity. What "Canadian" meant was not easy to define, except in terms of what it was not: American. On this, the French and British groups within Canada agreed. To cement the idea, the people of Quebec joined three other Canadian provinces (Ontario, Nova Scotia, and New Brunswick) in forming the Dominion of Canada. The new country was officially established when England ratified the British North American Act of 1867.

Quebec Joins the Industrial Revolution

The end of the Civil War in the United States and Quebec's membership in a greater and more stable Canada ushered in a new era of progress for the people of the province. Canada's first railway car, a coal-fired steam carriage, was built in Quebec by Henry Taylor in 1867. As the Quebec Central Railway was being constructed a few years later, blasting at Thetford revealed a rock that analysis showed to be asbestos, a fire-resistant mineral. By 1875 mining had begun, and the Eastern townships of Quebec became the major asbestos producers for the world. Government policy encouraged mining the bountiful minerals in the Canadian Shield, and soon Quebec was producing large amounts of coal, iron (which was first mined in 1730), copper, and nickel. The province also started to produce hydroelectricity to power its industries and cities.

Although Montreal had established public transport in the form of horse-drawn streetcars years before, the city's first

■ *Workers operate a large drill at an asbestos mine in Quebec. By the late nineteenth century, Quebec had become the largest asbestos producer in the world.*

electric streetcar, "The Rocket," went into service in 1892. This development was important because people could now build and live in suburbs, away from the hustle and bustle of the city and its factories.

Five years later, a Quebec City dentist, Henry Casgrain, brought a three-wheel motorized carriage—a "voiturette"—back from France and drove it around town at an alarming 18 miles per hour, signaling the beginning of the era of the private automobile. In the same year, he adapted it to the Quebec winter climate by replacing the front wheels with steel skis and the tire on the back wheel with a wooden rim studded with knobs—in effect making the first snowmobile.

Many in Quebec prospered, but while the English industrialists and railway builders made their fortunes, these were built upon high prices for goods and cheap (often French) labor. Those in government tended to be businessmen with no interest in labor reforms that would cut into their profits. Labor organizations in the skilled trades had been formed as early as 1812, but they were illegal. Striking for better working conditions or wages was also illegal and generally put down by the militia.

Yet conditions during the 1890s for the working poor of Quebec, most of whom were Frenchmen who had moved from their farms to the cities to find jobs in the new industries, were woeful. Laborers worked twelve-hour days, six days a week, for $12. That was not enough to survive and still pay the fare for the new electric streetcar, so they also had to live close to the factories. The only drinking water available came from wells that were next to the toilets. Laborers had neither paid holidays nor insurance against unemployment, accidents, or illness. These conditions were soon to lead to further discontent among the French in Quebec.

Entering the Twentieth Century

Despite these problems, Quebec continued to industrialize and become more urban as increasing numbers of farmers and rural folk moved to the cities looking for jobs. Canada, as part of the British empire, entered the First World War with Britain in 1914. The war had wide-ranging effects on Quebec. With many Canadian men fighting in Europe, women entered the workforce to supply Canadian and Allied forces with food and weapons. When the war ended, unemployment, high prices, and low wages resulted in the working men and women of Quebec joining other striking workers across the country to demand improvements.

■ *Canadian troops conduct a training exercise during World War I.*

Quebec's industrialization and urbanization continued through the 1920s and 1930s as the province developed its

■ French Resistance to World War I

French feelings of disconnection from English-speaking Canada came to the fore during World War I. At the outset, many French Canadians did not want to become involved in this "war to help Britain." During the first two years of the war, however, French Canadian protests were limited. The troops were all volunteer, and many of the battles were being fought on French soil to drive back invading Germans. Quebecois who did volunteer, such as the Royal Twenty-Second Regiment of Quebec, distinguished themselves in battle. By 1917, however, Canada's need for troops could no longer be met with volunteers, and the Canadian government called for a draft. The French in Quebec were strongly against the war by now, and they were joined by farmers, trade unions, and others across the country in resisting conscription. Over the short term the draft crisis of 1917 led to the election of a new (pro-draft) federal government. Over the long term it worsened the growing rift between French- and English-speaking Canadians.

natural resource industries, especially hydroelectric, logging for pulp and paper, and mining. The Second World War brought Quebec, as part of Canada, onto the world stage, not only as a fighting force but also as a supplier of raw materials and products for the allied war machine.

After World War II, Canada reduced its ties to Britain even further following investments made by American individuals and companies in Canada that totaled $10 billion by 1954. American companies now owned or controlled most of Canada's oil, gas, rubber, and automobile production; the majority of its nickel, iron, asbestos, and aluminum production; and over half of its pulp paper industry. The benefits to Quebec of short-range profits were obvious, but the long-term future for Quebec and the other provinces was not good, as the country, so shortly after freeing itself from British control, became increasingly dependent upon the United States.

"Long Live Free Québec"

Meanwhile, in Quebec, calls were being made not to free the province from the United States, but from the British-dominated Canada. In 1960, Jean Lesage became premier of Quebec and demanded that the province be allowed the freedom to exchange with other nations in matters of culture and education. Lesage's policies ushered in what has come to be called Quebec's "Quiet Revolution," a period of political and social reform that modernized Quebec society. New government ministries of education and cultural affairs took control of issues previously left to the church. Political patronage and corruption were attacked, and the voting age was lowered from twenty-one to eighteen. Lesage's government also nationalized the provincial electricity industry.

The renewed sense of purpose and pride in Quebec was also reflected in the growth of the Quebecois separatist movement during the 1960s. A radical group called the Front de Libération Quebecois (FLQ) decided to free Quebec through violent revolution if necessary and set off a bomb in Montreal in 1963. Many French Canadians supported the group's aims, if not its means. It was a more moderate separatist, René Lévesque, a journalist and then a minister in Lesage's government, who succeeded in jump-starting the movement when he brought several of the other separatist parties together to form the Parti Quebecois in 1968, with the purpose of achieving the same end through peaceful means. These separatist ambitions were fueled during the Expo 67 in Montreal when Charles de Gaulle, the French president, made a speech from a balcony at City Hall, in which he stated, "Long live Free Québec!"

■ *René Lévesque formed a separatist group called Parti Quebecois in 1968.*

Quebec independence seemed to receive another boost in 1968 when Pierre Trudeau, a French Canadian from Quebec, became prime minister of Canada. He was in favor of a strong federal government, but he made concessions to the French in his home province by pushing an act through Parliament in 1969 that made French the official second language for the country.

The FLQ felt Trudeau's actions were inadequate and so kidnapped a British diplomat and Quebec's Minister of Labor, demanding money and the release of imprisoned FLQ members. Trudeau responded by sending troops to Quebec, but they were unable to prevent the minister from being murdered. As a result of this atrocity, the FLQ began to lose popular support and it was soon dispersed by the federal government. At the same time, the federal government's use of troops, suspension of civil liberties, and attempts to equate terrorists with independence supporters alienated many Quebecois.

Separatism Stays on the Table

During the 1970s, the weakening economy and rising unemployment pushed the question of an independent Quebec to the back burner. When Lévesque finally won control of the Quebec government in 1976, he called for Quebec independence. Quebecers voted against separation, however, in the resulting 1980 referendum by a convincing 60–40 majority. An

■ Quebec's Love-Hate Relationship with Pierre Trudeau

Pierre Trudeau (1919–2000) was a key figure in Canadian and Quebec politics. He was a Quebecois who was prime minister of Canada from 1968 to 1979, a period that was marked by growing Quebecois efforts to separate from Canada. Trudeau was keenly aware of the centuries-old desire of French Canadians to maintain their culture and independence. Unlike many Quebecois, however, he thought that the best way to achieve this was to try to unite Canadians into a nation made up of many cultures. "One nation—one country," he declared. He wanted Quebecois to consider themselves Canadians, not French or English Canadians. But his idea ran counter to a growing demand among French Canadians for independence and a complete separation from the rest of Canada.

Trudeau had seen powerful local politicians in Quebec, in conjunction with schools and social programs dominated by the Roman Catholic Church, run roughshod over the rights of individuals. He feared a separate Quebec nation would result in more of the same. So his solution for keeping Quebec within Canada was to make Canada more bilingual, thereby including the Quebecois within Canada.

But in 1970, when Trudeau threw the might of the Canadian military against a small band of separatist terrorists in a heavy-handed show of force, he also undermined the individual rights and freedoms that he and his fellow Canadians professed to believe in. Trudeau went on to campaign against passage of the 1980 separatist referendum in Quebec. This further reduced his popularity among Quebecois. Trudeau will long be remembered by Canadians for his charisma and idealism, but he was not able to succeed in his fervent efforts to bring about a truly united Canada.

■ *Pierre Trudeau served as Canadian prime minister for eleven years.*

underlying fear was that the province might not do so well economically if it were to separate from the rest of the country. French Canadians were already among the poorest-paid workers in Quebec; their standard of living was 20 percent lower than their neighbors' in Ontario. Although Quebecers had agreed to stay within the greater Canada, the fundamental differences between French and English cultures were not resolved.

Life in Quebec Today

The French who came to the New World to live in Quebec shared the country with few other Europeans until the end of the eighteenth century, when an influx of English speakers accounted for 10 percent of Quebecers. Two hundred years later, of the more than seven million people living in Quebec, six million are descended from the original French settlers. Quebec's six million people of French origin have kept their language and culture intact even though they live on a continent where English is the language spoken by some three hundred million people and heard on almost all the airwaves. Travel to Quebec and one will find the French language everywhere—on street and shop signs, on radio and television, in homes and schools.

Quebecois share many aspects of everyday life with the average French person. Much as in France, Quebecois dine at bistros and fine restaurants where quality food is served in the tradition of great French cuisine. They speak the same language, of course, though the Quebecois have introduced the slight nasal twang to the language that Americans have to English, and to a certain extent the accents, idioms, and slang of the French are different from those of Quebec. The Quebecois, like the French, are tolerant and cosmopolitan, with the Quebecois having the reputation for being generally friendlier than the French, who characteristically are very reserved with foreigners.

But life in Quebec is not the same as life in France. The Quebecois have taken what they want of French—and English—

■ *Ninety percent of Quebec's residents speak French, a language seen on signs throughout the region.*

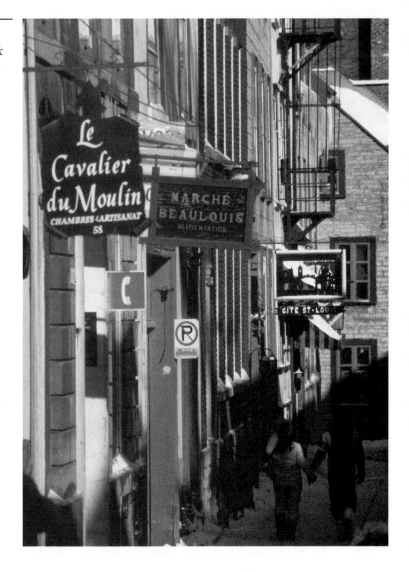

cultures and made their own synthesis, which could be called New World French.

The more than five hundred thousand English speakers in Quebec, on the other hand, who also trace their lineage back to early settlers, mostly now live in and around Montreal. More English Canadians in Quebec are bilingual than in the past—they must be to survive in an increasingly French-oriented province. But it is also possible for English-speaking Quebecers to put their children through an English-language school system, visit health care facilities where English is spoken, listen to radio stations beamed in from America, and watch American television programs.

Approximately seventy thousand Quebec residents descend from the original First Nations people. The remaining seven-hundred thousand people living in Quebec have arrived over the last century, and in greater numbers over the last two decades, mainly from Africa, Latin America, and Asia. These groups have enriched Quebec society with a wide range of new cuisines, music, and other cultural treasures that are giving Quebecers a look at life outside the European and American traditions in which they were raised.

More Religions, Fewer Practitioners

For centuries the Catholic Church has traditionally been very active in Quebec politics and education, as well as being the moral and spiritual authority for most Quebecers. But the last four decades have seen a dramatic shift in Quebec households

■ *A traditional Catholic church in the heart of Montreal. Most Quebecois consider themselves Catholic, but few actually practice their religion.*

and society. While close to nine out of ten Quebecers still consider themselves Catholics, few of them attend weekly mass or are active in the Church. Statistics suggest that only 10 to 20 percent of Catholic Quebecois practice their religion today compared to 95 percent before 1960.

While the decision not to participate in the Church has been an individual one in each case, the lessened support is at least partly due to the gradual decline of the Church as a public force since the 1960s. Quebec, under the leadership of Jean Lesage at this time, began to move health, social services, and other aspects of public life away from church influence. The Catholic Church's restrictive views on social issues such as abortion and gay rights may also be contributing to its loss of influence on Quebecois, who are generally known for their liberal social views.

In Quebec today, the larger proportion of practicing Catholics is made up of recent immigrants who, like most other immigrants from Champlain onwards, have brought their religious beliefs with them. With the large influx of immigrants in the late twentieth century, Quebec has seen a sudden blossoming of other religions, such as Islam, Hinduism, and Buddhism. Adherents may make up approximately 10 percent of the populace, but their numbers have been growing rapidly.

Changing Roles for Families and Women

Beyond religious affiliation, the makeup of the families in which Quebecers are raised has changed over the last few decades. The 3 percent annual growth rate in population kicked off by Louis XIV has fallen dramatically today—between 1996 and 2001 the province experienced the lowest census-to-census growth rate in its history. (Quebec's population did grow slightly, unlike the economically depressed maritime provinces that actually lost population.) Part of the problem in Quebec is the weakening of the family as a social unit. In 1998, for instance, while there were some twenty-four thousand marriages in the province, there were also seventeen thousand divorces, yielding a ratio of divorces to marriages that is much higher than in any other province. One in five Quebec households with children has only one parent, usually the mother. As in other parts of Canada, women have joined the workforce and postponed raising a family to later years. The large families once so characteristic of Catholic households (to this day official Church policy frowns upon most forms of birth control) are rarely seen in Quebec. Some 85 percent of the almost one million families in Quebec have only one or two children.

■ *A Quebec business-woman works on her computer. Women in Quebec enjoy a wider variety of career opportunities than in years past.*

Economic factors may also be contributing to the trend toward smaller families. Quebec's economy has fluctuated in recent years, but in general it has suffered in comparison with Ontario's. Nearly one in four Quebec families is considered low-income by the Canadian government's definition of more than 70 percent of income spent on housing, food, and clothes.

On the plus side of the ledger, life for women in Quebec has seen definite improvements. While Canadian women were allowed to vote for the first time in federal elections in 1917, the Catholic Church prevented women from voting in Quebec until 1940, making them the last women in North America to be enfranchised. Whereas in the past working women were mainly found in the fields of education and health, today they are as likely as men to play key roles in business, the arts, politics, and other fields.

In the meantime, the number of Quebecers over 65 has increased from 6 percent in 1961 to 12 percent in 1996. As with other industrialized nations, these grandparents and older folks for the most part are not living with their children but are on their own or in homes for the elderly.

A Public and Private School System

As is to be expected, school is mandatory for all children, beginning from age six at least until age sixteen. High school ends with grade twelve, after which students may attend publicly-funded junior colleges for two years, earning a diploma before they apply to university. Outside its public school system, Quebec has a widely used dual-school system

■ Montreal: A World-Class City

Montreal is a thriving, international city that is home to more than one million people and tens of thousands of businesses of all sizes. It is the second-largest French-speaking city in the world (after Paris) and the driving force behind the Quebec economy. Within Canada as a whole, Montreal's metropolitan area is second only to Toronto's in terms of size and influence. With regard to quality of life for its residents, however, Montreal considers itself second to no city in the world. Indeed, one recent study ranked Montreal, along with Seattle and Melbourne, as one of the most livable cities in the world. Montreal is deservedly world famous for its modern subway system, availability of free health care and education, and respect for the natural environment.

The breadth of the city's cultural activities is remarkable. The Montreal Symphony Orchestra, the Canadian Ballet, the Montreal International Jazz Festival, the Montreal Opera, and the Montreal World Film Festival are some of the arts activities that Quebecers can enjoy. Sports fans can watch the National Hockey League Canadiens play in the gleaming new Molson Centre. Formula One cars race through a city-street course in an annual event, as do high-tech bicycles in another. For those wanting something more colorful still, there is a fireworks competition at La Ronde in the late spring.

Montreal has hosted several international events over the last few decades. The World's Fair Expo in 1967 attracted fifty million visitors in celebration of Canada's Centennial. The Summer Olympic Games were held nine years later in a park that had been set aside half a century earlier for just that purpose. And four years after that, Montreal was the site of the International Floral Exposition.

Of course, Montreal is not a paradise. It has many of the same everyday problems found in other big cities—traffic jams, noise, auto pollution, and crime. (Overall, the province's violent crime rate is the lowest in Canada.) But Montrealers have created a city that has both the class and flair of the French and the gregariousness of the American people, which is why it ranks with Paris, London, and New York as one of the best cities to visit. For Montrealers who live there, of course, it's life as usual.

servicing some 130,000 students. Most of these attend French-speaking Catholic schools. Protestant schools, on the other hand, are predominantly English-speaking. The Quebec government pays 55 percent of the expenses of running these schools compared with 84 percent of the fees for public schools, with the balance coming from local property taxes.

The high-achieving top one-quarter of Quebec's students spend fifteen years or longer in the education system, moving

from preschool to postgraduate university studies. Approximately 87 percent of Quebec students complete secondary school and 39 percent obtain a diploma of college studies. The dropout rate in Quebec's schools, however, is higher than in most other provinces, and Quebec also has a relatively high number of individuals with a grade eight education or less. Quebec thus also suffers from a lower rate of overall literacy than Canada as a whole.

■ Students at a private girls school in Montreal. Quebec's private school system, composed mostly of French-speaking Catholic schools, is a popular alternative to public schools.

An Economy in Transition

Quebec's economy in recent years has been undergoing a change from one based on manufacturing jobs to a service- and knowledge-based one. Between 1990 and 1997, job growth in Quebec for knowledge-based work increased 2.1 percent, the same as in the rest of Canada. The number of jobs in the manufacturing sector and other jobs (such as forestry and farming) fell by 0.5 percent in Quebec compared to a growth of 1 percent in Canada.

As Quebec economists André Desnoyers and Yves Lirette have noted:

> Since the 1980s, the computer science-communications-information nexus has developed at an astounding rate and is generating a greater need for versatile workers who have advanced knowledge. Information is becoming a direct factor of production and its immediate accessibility

is fuelling its development. There is a relative shift from jobs in the traditional sectors (primary, manufacturing, and construction) to the service sector which is still going on today. In tandem with job losses in the traditional sectors (productivity losses or gains), we are witnessing the rise of new industries such as software, computers, multimedia, and microelectronics.[10]

For young people who acquired the necessary schooling and training to work at high-tech jobs, the news is good. For those who did not do well in their education and are joining the workforce as store clerks and fast-food cooks, the news is not so good. Half of these new positions offer only part-time employment. And taxes in Quebec, which has Canada's highest provincial personal income tax rate, take a significant bite out of paychecks. Middle-class families earning approximately

■ Quebec City: Where Old and New Worlds Meet

While Montreal is a fun-loving cosmopolitan city, Quebec (often called Quebec City) is a romantic collection of four-century-old houses, ancient citadels and churches, and winding streets. Quebec City is perched on a palisade that juts out into the St. Lawrence River. It is the only walled city north of Mexico and was the first city in North America to be placed on the World Heritage list of treasured natural wonders and human-made structures. Quebec City is an ancient treasure, too, by North American standards—it was founded twelve years before the pilgrims landed in Plymouth, Massachusetts.

Most noticeable about Quebec City, however, is that all but 5 percent of its inhabitants trace their ancestors back to France, so there is no question that French is king in this ancient and elegant city. Much like the French-influenced city of New Orleans with its Mardi Gras, Quebec City holds the ten-day Carnaval de Quebec in February to celebrate the approaching end of winter and to live it up before Lent (when Catholics are meant to restrict eating, drinking, and pleasures for 40 days). The people of Quebec City are as romantic as their city and as fun-loving as their Montreal neighbors. Even when snow falls and the temperature plummets, they can be found out in the streets, cheering on the sparkling parades, watching fireworks, and admiring the ice sculptures. And come summer, the people of Quebec City celebrate Le Festival d'Été de Québec (Quebec's Summer Festival), which is the largest event dedicated to French culture in North America.

$55,000 per year may see more than 50 percent of their income diverted to various taxes in Quebec, which is slightly higher than the rate for Canada as a whole. The result is a standard of living in Quebec that by the late 1990s was 10 percent lower than that of the average Canadian.

The economic challenges Quebec faces are also affecting most other industrialized societies. Overall, Quebec citizens still enjoy one of the highest standards of living in the world. In the last quarter of a century, the number of Quebecers who have started their own businesses has increased to 15 percent, and many older Quebecers are taking early retirement to enjoy the fruits of their labors. The reality is that facing challenges is not a new condition for Quebecers. Instead of the challenge being the harsh outdoors environment, it is now how to survive in a changing economic landscape.

■ *Quebec City residents enjoy the festivities during the city's annual Winter Carnival.*

Quebec City is perhaps the only city on the continent to offer the old-world charm of Europe, rather than a modern-day replica. For its inhabitants, it is as close as anyone in North America can get to living in France, without actually being there. "It is a place not to be forgotten or mixed up in the mind with other places," said the English author Charles Dickens, "or altered for a moment in the crowd of scenes a traveler can recall."

Quebec still has a wealth of natural resources, too, from minerals to forestry products, as well as many very strong high-tech industries such as aerospace, pharmaceuticals, information technology, telecommunications, hydroelectricity, and metallurgy. These can continue to produce enough products for consumption inside and outside Quebec so that the province will be able to maintain its high standard of living. And for those who persevere with their schooling, good jobs will always be available.

A Lively Political Scene

Most people in Quebec, like America, do not spend their time immersed in politics, but come election time, many do care enough about how their city, province, or country are run to go out and cast their vote. In the United States, if half the eligible voters actually do so, it is considered a good turnout. No less than 94 percent of eligible Quebecers, on the other hand, cast their votes in the 1995 referendum on separation, and Quebec tied New Brunswick as the provinces with the greatest percentage of eligible voters casting ballots in the 1997 federal election.

The political system is similar to that of the British. The capitol of the federal government, with its House of Commons and Senate, is located in Ottawa, Ontario, just across

■ *The changing of the guard at Parliament Hill in Ottawa, home of the Canadian Senate and House of Commons. Come election time, most people in Quebec get involved in the political process.*

Quebec's western border. The federal government deals with and coordinates external affairs, national defense, and monetary policy for all ten provinces. Quebec's provincial government, however, can act upon a wide range of issues, including education, health care, immigration, and the use of its own natural resources. Quebec also has the right to send official representatives to countries around the world for cultural and trade purposes. (Canadian provinces have far more autonomy than the states in the United States.) Not surprisingly, among Canadian provinces, Quebec leads the way in insisting upon its right to represent itself abroad.

A Tradition of Public Health Care

Quebec, like the other Canadian provinces, offers extensive public-supported health services. In addition to providing universal and continuous health care for all citizens, free of charge, the goverment has mobile services visit remote areas to ensure all Quebecers are looked after properly. One in every ten Quebecers works in the health care sector, making it a major employer in the province.

While all citizens are eligible for these government/tax-funded health services, the underfunding of the system over the years, and widespread closing of hospitals and health facilities at the end of the 1990s in a drive to become more efficient, have resulted in long waits for care in many places. Stories abound of patients waiting six months or longer for an operation or for a high-tech diagnostic procedure. Quebecers nevertheless remain committed to a health care system that is accessible, universal, and government-supported. A recent survey found 93 percent of Quebecers want any budget surplus spent to ensure health care remains free.

Another indicator that the Quebec health care system is experiencing financial difficulties is the refusal of some Ontario health facilities to accept Quebec health care cards because the Quebec government is either slow in paying or pays less than the full charge. One result of this financial strain is that a two-tier system, with those able to pay for care going to the front of the line, is starting to appear in Quebec. This is especially evident in areas such as home care and physiotherapy.

Guaranteeing the Basics

All in all, the residents of Quebec enjoy a high standard of living, with education, including universities, and health care covered. The educational system struggles in some places to prevent students from dropping out, which is leading to a lower standard of living for too high a number of young people. But public funding covers special assistance for the poor and comprehensive programs for the elderly so that most people still have a basic standard of living guaranteed. Beyond this the government of Quebec also places much emphasis on supporting the province's unique culture.

A Culture Alive

Q uebec's seven million inhabitants have created an extremely rich and dynamic culture that is recognized the world over for its creative theater, music, dance, cinema, literature, and visual arts. Much of this success is due to the rich intermingling of French and English history, culture, and language. Few other areas in the world offer such a unique background to inspire the creative process.

Quebec's lively culture also benefits from the active encouragement and financial backing of the provincial government—which, of course, means Quebecers as a whole agreeing to the spending of their tax dollars on cultural activities. Since the early 1960s, Quebec artists have been able to take advantage of government grants to gain training and to produce and disseminate their works. Provincial support has also enabled hundreds of arts organizations, libraries, museums, bookstores, art galleries, exhibition centers, and concert halls to be established, and numerous arts festivals to be sponsored.

Quebec's culture is not exclusively so high-minded, however. The province is also known for all sorts of rambunctious winter sports, from ice hockey to snowmobiling. Montreal, Quebec City, and other cities host a variety of exciting events, from auto races to a comedy festival. And lest we forget, it was two Quebec journalists, Chris Haney and Scott Abbott, who invented the game Trivial Pursuit in their Montreal kitchen in 1979.

■ *An artist works and displays paintings for sale in Montreal.*

Readers and Writers

Quebec enjoys a lively literary scene, especially in the major cities. Perhaps because of the province's long, cold winters, reading and discussing books has become a favorite pastime for Quebecers. Approximately three out of every five people of the province consider themselves regular book readers. Much of this reading is applied to books written by Quebecers, who author some six thousand published works each year, a high volume given the province's total population.

Among Quebec's most notable authors is the "beat generation" novelist Jack Kerouac (1922–1969). Although he is known as an American writer, he was born Jean Louis Lebris de Kerouac to French Canadian parents who had recently migrated to the mill town of Lowell, Massachusetts, from Quebec. According to critic Mark Fellows, "Like his brother Francis Gerard and sister Caroline, Jack would attend St. Louis of France parochial school, where English was taught as a second language. [Jack's mother] Gabrielle Kerouac ran her household in French, and even at age 18 one of the more influential American novelists of the twentieth century was far from fluent in English."[11] Fellows also makes the point that Kerouac's childhood background as a French Canadian Catholic had important influences on his work.

Another Quebec author who has built a reputation for the province as a source of excellent literature is screenwriter, essayist, and novelist Mordecai Richler (1931–2001). His 1959 novel *The Apprenticeship of Duddy Kravitz,* noted critic Russell Brown, "is really the beginning of Canadian literature as a body of literature. Before that we had Canadian writers . . . [but] Richler was really the first of the beginning of that explosion of new writing and especially new novels that told us about our time and place."[12] An outspoken Anglophone, Richler was a controversial figure in Quebec and most Quebecois were critical of him while he was alive. Perhaps Quebec novelist Jacques Godbout was right when he noted, upon Richler's recent death, "I believe that he's a great man, an irreplaceable man and I think that Quebecers will regret the fact that they won't have him to kick around anymore."[13]

Enjoying and Creating Art

Quebec offers a wide range of cultural activities, such as visiting the province's almost five hundred museums and enjoying some of the two thousand live theater performances each year. On average, one in five Quebecers visits an art museum or arts and crafts fair each year, quite a high figure compared, for example, to the United States. Quebecers spend almost a thousand dollars each on average buying products at those fairs.

Quebecers are not just spectators, but also participants. One in ten, for instance, takes arts courses or workshops or belongs to an artistic or cultural club or association. One person in three spends five hours a week doing volunteer work, and one in eight goes beyond tax dollar support of Quebec's culture by making personal donations.

Those Quebecers who live in more remote areas, or who have less desire to go out to cultural events, tend to derive their entertainment from television viewing, averaging about three hours a day, with their favorite programs being newscasts and public affairs programs, followed by films, humor, soap operas, and miniseries. The French network of the Canadian Broadcasting System provides French-content programming for Quebec and most parts of the country. Naturally, most Quebecers watch some television—about two-thirds of Quebec households have two television sets and many Quebecers are cable subscribers—and almost all residents listen to music on the radio.

A large majority of Quebecers takes the time to go out and enjoy their culture, the most popular destinations being

■ *A tour guide addresses a group of visitors to the Montreal Biodome, one of Quebec's many museums.*

■ Reinventing the Circus

Anyone who has seen the exhilarating and highly inventive performances of Cirque du Soleil cannot be anything but impressed and enchanted. The performances bring together circus acrobatics, ballet, theater, sometimes driving and sometimes ethereal music, choreography, and fantastic, original costume and set designs into a nonstop, jaw-dropping spectacle—truly a Circus of the Sun.

The idea for Cirque du Soleil was born in 1985, when a group of Montreal street performers joined forces to found the "High-Heels Club," named after the stilts that most of them walked on. With other acts including fire eating, juggling, and music, they created a street festival in a town that had no real tradition of circuses. But their goal was to bring together the circus arts, theater, and fantasy. They also decided from the start not to feature elephants and other animals, which have sometimes been mistreated in other circuses.

Their resulting performances immediately caught on, first in Montreal, then Quebec, and then the rest of North America, Europe, and Asia. In 2001 some six million spectators saw any of half a dozen different Cirque du Soleil performances with exotic titles like La Nouba, Saltimbanco, and Dralion either at resident locations in Las Vegas and Walt Disney World in Orlando or at various tour locations around the world. Circus schools in Montreal and Quebec City now train young people to join the profession. What the Quebec performers began in 1985 and Cirque du Soleil has done since is to completely reinvent and revitalize the circus, bringing it into the twenty-first century.

■ *Cirque du Soleil contortionists perform in Montreal.*

cinemas (with popular Hollywood imports often being shown either dubbed in French or with French subtitles), followed by shows in clubs, nightclubs or bars, and dance halls. Comedy shows, theater performances, and concerts also attract large audiences.

A Sporting People

While intellectual and cultural pursuits are popular in Quebec, they face stiff competition for the hearts and minds of

Quebecers from various sports and recreational pursuits. One survey suggested that interest in reading and cultural activities has grown recently and that the amount of time spent watching television and listening to the radio has decreased, with the extra time being spent on sports. Three in every five Quebecers spend at least a quarter of their leisure time engaged in physical exercise or games.

A love of sports is in the blood of Quebecers. The Algonquin Indians, for instance, developed lacrosse. Quebecers even contributed to American football, as the first organized game ever played took place in Cambridge, Massachusetts, between Harvard University and Montreal's McGill University in 1874. This game changed the sport of football as it had been played until then, from one based on soccer to one based on the English game of rugby. While the American game of football evolved over the decades further away from its English roots, in Quebec (and the rest of Canada) football has maintained closer ties to rugby. Canadian football uses a rounder ball and is played on a larger field than the American version. Canadian football also involves more kicking of the ball.

Given the wide variety of physical activities available in the region's great outdoors, this love of sports is not surprising. With a million pristine lakes and rivers in which to row, paddle, swim, white-water raft, jet ski, powerboat and model boat, sail, windsurf, and fish, there's something for everybody to do during the summer. Every conceivable sport and activity can be and is played out in the vast Canadian Shield, from hunting to rock climbing, hiking to spelunking (cave exploring). Many of the cities have set aside walkways and trails for biking and skating. In southern Quebec, "Le Petit Train du

■ *Students play a game of Canadian football at Montreal's McGill University.*

Nord" (Small Train of the North) is a 125-mile (200-kilometer) biking and hiking (and, in winter, cross-country skiing) path that passes through more than a dozen towns and villages. It attracts a steady flow of day-users and week-long bikers and trekkers from within Quebec and from afar, all attracted by the scenery and the many galleries, shops, and bistros in the local villages. After enduring a long, hard winter, Quebecers eagerly take advantage of the warm, sunlit days.

Quebecers, of course, are also enthusiastic supporters and spectators at a variety of sporting events, many of them world-class. The Montreal Expos (named after Expo 67, the World's Fair held in Montreal) were admitted into Major League Baseball's National League in 1968. The Expos, along with Toronto's Blue Jays, helped popularize "America's pastime" in Canada. Unfortunately for Quebec's many baseball fans, the Expos' relatively low revenue stream from radio and television has caused the team to fall into the group of "small-market" teams struggling to compete (and, in the case of the Expos, possibly even survive more than a few more years).

For racing enthusiasts, there is the annual Canadian Formula One Grand Prix and the Players Atlantic Formula Grand Prix, which attract contestants and spectators from around the world. Every June almost 50,000 bicyclists flood Montreal to take part in the world's largest amateur cycling event, the Tour de L'île, which winds for 37 miles (60 kilometers) around Montreal Island. The annual powerboat regatta that has been held since 1938 in Salaberry-de-Valleyfield, located 30 miles (48 kilometers) south of Montreal on the St. Lawrence River, attracts thousands of spectators and has given the area a reputation as "the world capital of powerboat racing." For those who prefer a more sedately paced water race, there is the International Swimming Marathon, an annual 24-

■ *Thousands of spectators from around the world attend the annual Canadian Formula One Grand Prix.*

mile (32-kilometer) swim from Piekouagami to Roberval across Lake St. Jean north of Quebec City. A recently instituted ocean race commemorates the 450th anniversary of Jacques Cartier's arrival in North America, with ships racing in the only non-solo, east-to-west sailing event, from Saint Malo in France to Quebec.

A History of Winter Sports

As much as Quebecers love their outdoor sports during the spring, summer, and fall months, it is the winter sports that are the closest to the hearts (and muscles) of Quebecers. To understand why, it helps to know some local history. With most traffic from the outside world moving along rivers until the nineteenth century, winters tended to become one long holiday as the rivers froze over, leaving Quebecers with little to do except pass the time and enjoy themselves. Sleighing was one way. British officers garrisoned in Quebec often ended up in snowbanks because they were not used to controlling a sleigh, but they had "muffins" to keep them company—warm and cheerful young women sitting beside them. "Muffinage" was a desirable status because it often led to marriage.

British soldiers introduced curling in 1759, causing one Quebec farmer to complain: "Today, I saw a bunch of Scotsmen throwing huge iron balls, like canon balls [along the ice], then yelling 'Soupe, soupe' [Scottish pronunciation for 'sweep, sweep'], then laughing like fools. They *are* fools!"[14] Curling remains a popular winter sport in Quebec, which has numerous indoor and outdoor ice courts. Of course, it is now played not with cannon balls but with highly polished, heavy flat-bottomed stones. The object is for a four-member team to slide the stone as close as possible to the center of a target area. Canadian teams have become powerful competitors in this sport, which was added to the Winter Olympics in 2002.

In years past, when Quebecers weren't racing their horses along the frozen rivers, they were pushing flat-bottomed, triangular boats over the ice. Toboggans were often seen shooting down steep hills, and the Montreal Snowshoe Club would head out even in blizzards for their exercise, clicking along at a steady pace in single file, blankets around their shoulders and singing loudly. For variety they would indulge in torch-lit parades, snowball battles, and highland dances. For the less boisterous, as well as the ladies, there was ice skating to waltzes and mazurkas at Montreal's gaslit Victoria Rink. European immigrants brought skating to Canada in the mid-nineteenth century, with the first race apparently being held on the St. Lawrence River. The Quebecers even put together

North America's first Winter Carnival, held in Montreal in 1833. It featured five days of curling, sleigh races, tobogganing, snowshoeing, hockey, skating, and fireworks.

Winter Sports Continue to Boom

Fast-forwarding to today, we find the winter sports tradition alive and well. Ice skating and hockey draw huge and enthusiastic crowds to the ice rinks in every town and precinct. After Gaetan Boucher won gold medals in the 1,000-meter and 1,500-meter speed-skating races at the 1984 Olympics, a new sport was added as many Quebecers modeled themselves on Quebec's latest hero.

Although one man skied from Montreal to Quebec in 1879 using nine-foot skis and one pole, it was many years before skiing caught on. Today, however, a million serious and casual skiers and snowboarders hit the eight hundred runs at the one hundred alpine ski resorts around the province, some open half the year thanks to the use of hundreds of (predominantly Quebec-made) snowmaking machines.

Even more impressive, one and a half million Quebecers can be found skiing gracefully along the thousands of miles of marked and groomed cross-country ski trails throughout the province, both in the middle of cities and across national parks, where heated cabins are provided along the way. In the United States by comparison, there are far more downhill skiers than cross-country skiers, and relatively few cross-country ski trails.

No list of Quebec's winter sports would be complete without mentioning the snowmobile, whose modern history really began in 1959 when Quebec innovator Joseph Bombardier perfected the first assembly-line-produced machine. (The Bombardier Company's Ski-Doo model remains a bestselling snowmobile.) In recent years the snowmobile has become a vital means of transport in the villages of central and northern Quebec. It is also used for sports and recreation in the south, where almost 20,000 miles (32,000 kilometers) of well-marked trails are dotted with hotels, restaurants, gas stations, and repair shops, and patrolled by snowmobile-based police patrols. For the real diehards, there is the annual international Raid des Braves competition, a race over almost 2,000 miles (3,200 kilometers) of ungroomed trails in the north.

Other winter activities that are peculiar to Quebec and some other northern climes, but not engaged in by too many Quebecers, include dogsledding and ice fishing. While a few hardy people enjoy these activities, there are many Quebecers who opt for exercising their brain cells, instead of their muscles, in the pursuit of the arts.

A Culture That Encourages Creativity

Among Quebec's many painters, photographers, and cinematographers is the world-renowned Armenian-born photographer Yousuf Karsh, who as a child went to school in Sherbrooke, Quebec. He opened his portrait studio in Ottawa during 1932 and has been photographing world leaders and celebrities ever since. His 1941 photograph of Winston Churchill, the prime minister of Great Britain during World

■ *Quebecers partici-*
pate in a cross-country
skiing competition.
Cross-country skiing
is one of Quebec's most
popular winter sports.

■ Montreal's Vibrant Underground

One way to escape the bitter winters in Montreal is to take a three-month vacation in Bermuda every year. As tempting as this may be for most, it's not a realistic alternative for those who need to live and work in the city year-round. A more practical approach for residents and visitors alike is to make like gophers and use Montreal's amazing "la ville souterraine" (underground city).

In Montreal, eighteen miles of climate-controlled underground tunnels, pedestrian concourses, and mural-decorated subway stations provide a comfortable option to topside travel. This "parallel subterranean universe," as one guidebook has described it, opens in various places into huge mall-like complexes. Overall, one has access to more than twelve hundred shops, boutiques, restaurants, fast-food counters, banks, movie theaters, hotels, and apartment complexes. Many Quebecers take advantage of the brightly lit and clean underground passageways, or the quiet, rubber-wheeled underground trains, to shop and go about their business without once stepping outside into freezing temperatures, sleet, and snow. Montreal was the first city to create an underground city, the earliest section being opened at Place Ville-Marie (a building development) in 1966. La ville souterraine continues to grow, more or less haphazardly, as new buildings and stations add connections. Other cold-weather cities in Quebec and elsewhere have copied the idea, although not on such a grand scale.

■ *Montreal's vast underground city bustles with activity.*

War II, brought Karsh recognition internationally for his ability to capture the expression that typified his subject. Karsh caught the exact scowl he was looking for in Churchill, for instance, by snatching the cigar that almost always stuck out of his mouth and then snapping the picture of the prime minister's angry reaction.

In film, since the early 1970s the Canadian government has taken steps to free the nation of Hollywood dominance by requiring that 60 percent of the programming on Canadian television be written and/or performed by Canadians, and 30 percent for radio. The result has been a rapid growth of Canadian film and music production, especially in Quebec.

If there is a national art in Canada, it could be said to be film, with Montreal as a major hub for the industry. The National Film Board owns the most documentary film studios in the world, many in Quebec, and is also the focus for a thriving animation industry that is regarded highly throughout the world. Between animation and documentaries, Canadians win an average of seventy international film prizes every year.

Montreal's World Film Festival has highlighted the excellent work of many Canadian directors, most of whose films, being thoughtful and socially conscious, are unlike typical Hollywood fare. The drama *The Red Violin* recently proved very popular in the United States. Another strength in Quebec film is in the realm of special effects—its studios and facilities have been used to shoot scenes in such films as *Jurassic Park* and *Titanic.*

A Song on Their Lips

The troubadours of old, following centuries of singing tradition in France, are well represented in Quebec today by popular writers, composers, and performers. Leonard Cohen, the Montreal-born poet and singer, brought out his first album in 1968, for instance, and has remained a prominent artist into the new century. Celine Dion, a Quebecois, established her reputation worldwide as a premier vocalist in the 1990s.

These stars shine in the popular culture, while no fewer than one hundred other musical organizations cater to the demand for live classical music. The Montreal Symphony Orchestra, under the baton of Charles Dutoit, is one of the foremost orchestras in the world, but it is only one among ten in the province. Two opera companies and numerous ballet and dance companies, from the classical Les Grands Ballets Canadiens to contemporary groups such as O Vertigo Dance, attract many Quebecers

■ Just for Laughs

Montreal has earned the title of "Humor Capital of the World" thanks to the unique "Juste pour Rire" (Just for Laughs) Festival. It began in 1982 as a two-night comedy show in French and grew quickly into an eleven-day festival each July that pretty well engulfs the whole city in laughter. In 2000 almost nine hundred comedians from fifteen countries had audience members in stitches at more than two thousand performances in English and French. The festival has become so popular that it is broadcast around the world to millions of television viewers.

Famous comedians who have performed at Just for Laughs include Jerry Seinfeld, Canadian-born Jim Carrey, Rowan "Mr. Bean" Atkinson, George Burns, and Monty Python's Graham Chapman. Many comedians have become famous after coming to public attention at the festival, as have other performers, such as the British percussion ensemble STOMP, which has not looked back since its 1992 performance. Likewise, Australia's Tap Dogs leaped to stardom after its 1996 performance at Just for Laughs.

A highlight of the festival is the World Improv Championships in which four teams representing Eastern Canada, Western Canada, Ontario, and Quebec make up the comedy as they interact with one another. In a world where depressing and terrible things happen too often, Quebec's Just for Laughs manages to bring cheer to many.

and others to their spellbinding and graceful performances. Together with the 250 professional theater companies in the province, there is no doubt that Quebecers have a thriving cultural scene quite out of proportion to their numbers.

Nowhere is the popularity of music more pronounced and evident than in the many outdoor music festivals that the Quebecers cram into their too-short summers. The International Lanaudière Festival came together in 1978 in the town of Joliette, a short distance north of Montreal, a collaboration between several local music schools and choruses, three youth orchestras, and the Montreal Symphony Orchestra. In subsequent years, stars like Frederica von Stade, Rudolf Nureyev, Itzhak Perlman, Mstislav Rostropovich, and Sir Neville Marriner have joined artists from many other countries to perform at events for two months straight. Similarly the city of Victoriaville hosts a five-day, twenty-five concert program of avant garde music, including improvised jazz, multimedia, and "sonic experiments" that draws thousands of aficionados from around the world to their small town.

The Quebec City Summer Festival caters especially to Quebecois families, attracting upwards of 200,000 children among its annual crowd of 700,000. They are entertained by some 400 performers from 20 countries. The festival began in 1968 when seven young artists and a group of businessmen were looking for a way to liven up city squares and parks and to promote French music and other arts. In four months and

■ Quebec's Bilingual International Pop Star

Celine Dion was born in 1968 in Charlemagne, a small town 30 miles (48 kilometers) east of Montreal, the youngest of 14 children. Her parents were both musicians and operated a small club in which every family member, at one time or another, performed to entertain the customers. Celine joined her family at these performances when she was five, singing "Mamy Blue" at the wedding of one of her brothers.

At age twelve, Dion composed a French song, "It Was Only a Dream," with the help of her mother and one of her brothers. In 1981 a demo tape containing this song came to the attention of music manager René Angelil. He was so convinced Dion would become a top star that he mortgaged his house to finance the recording of Celine's first album. The next year, she won the Gold Medal at the Yamaha World Song Festival in Tokyo and the Musician's Award for Top Performer.

In 1983 Dion became the first Canadian to receive a Gold Record in France. She grew up speaking French, of course, but learned English by the late 1980s to increase her appeal to the English-speaking markets. In 1991 she won international acclaim and her stardom was assured when she recorded the title track for Disney's *Beauty and the Beast,* which went to number one on the pop charts and earned Academy and Grammy Awards. Since then, she has recorded more than a dozen albums with total sales in excess of 100 million copies worldwide. Dion's recordings achieved what those of few other French speakers have been able to do: appeal to both French, Canadian, and English audiences, earning awards and topping charts in all three countries.

In 1994, after seven years of dating, Dion married Angelil, who is twenty-six years older than her. After touring extensively through the 1990s, Celine took off almost two years to be with her new child and to nurse René through a bout of cancer. Her many fans eagerly embraced her return to live performing in 2002, and the release of her *A New Day Has Come* album.

■ *Pop star Celine Dion hails from Quebec.*

■ *A jazz band performs at the eleven-day Montreal International Jazz Festival.*

with $17,000 in funds, they managed to present 50 performances. These were a hit, and the rest, as they say, is history.

But when it comes to music festivals in Quebec, the king has to be the Montreal International Jazz Festival. This eleven-day festival began in 1980 and now attracts almost two million people to the city. They come to see the jazz greats perform at three hundred outdoor events. Among the favorite performers has been Montreal-born jazz pianist Oscar Peterson, an African Canadian who learned from his father, a self-taught pianist working as a railway porter. Peterson won a national competition organized by the just-formed Canadian Broadcasting Corporation when he was fourteen and by the early 1940s was appearing regularly on nationally broadcast weekly radio shows. He has gone on to win popular and critical acclaim as well as numerous awards, including seven Grammy nods for performances and, in 1997, a "Lifetime Achievement" Grammy.

From the perspective of children in Quebec today, Oscar Peterson's youth may have taken place in the dim recesses of history, but his story is their story, too. The culture of Quebec today is increasingly supportive of any Quebecer who has something to say and the skill to say it in a creative way. How successfully Quebec can continue to support the young, the old, the talented, and the artistic, however, depends upon whether it can rise to the challenges that face it as it enters the twenty-first century.

Looking for Solutions

M ention Quebec and the issue that comes to mind first for most people is the province's ongoing debate over whether to separate from the rest of Canada. The separatist movement has been unfolding since the 1960s, but it is hardly the only concern for many of the people of Quebec today. The province has a number of pressing problems to contend with, including adapting to the new global economy, dealing with environmental concerns, developing as an increasingly multicultural society, and responding to First Nations' land claims. At the same time, because the separatist movement is based on a deep-seated desire to maintain a unique culture and identity, rather than just become another piece in the English-speaking, American cultural jigsaw, it is likely to remain a force to be dealt with for some time.

A Population in Flux

The challenges Quebec faces today must be considered in light of the ongoing shifts in the province's population. For example, as is the case in most industrialized nations, the population of Quebec is aging. Demographers project that within three decades Quebec will have one of the oldest populations among industrialized societies. In 1996 roughly one in every eight Quebecers was aged sixty-five or over. If present trends continue, by 2031 the ratio will be almost one in three, with many of the elderly over age eighty.

■ *Quebec's aging popu-*
lation is likely to have
serious long-term
effects on the province's
economy.

The effect of an aging population on the provincial economy is a major long-term concern. Eventually the province
may have too few young people available to work to produce
the wealth needed to support a high standard of living. Fewer
workers mean the government collects less revenue from pay-
roll taxes. This can lead to shortfalls in government funding
of public health care and retirement programs, which in turn
need larger and larger amounts of money to pay for benefits
due the elderly. The most obvious solutions—reducing social
benefits to the elderly or raising taxes on young workers—are
politically unpopular.

The aging trend in Quebec is due to a number of factors,
including a very low birth rate and an effective health care system that helps increase the average life expectancy. The birth
rate of 1.5 children for each Quebec woman of childbearing
age is second only to Germany as the lowest rate in the Western world, and falls below the rate of 2.1 children per mother
that is needed just to maintain the existing population level.
(Although Quebec's population increased by approximately
one million residents from 1981 to 1996, from 1996 to 2001
Quebec's population increased by only 100,000 persons, a 1.4
percent growth rate.) Because King Louis XIV's seventeenth-
century solution to ship young women from France is no

longer feasible, in the 1970s the Quebec government under Premier Robert Bourassa tried another method: offering taxpayers a $500 bonus for the first child, $1,000 for the second, and $6,000 for each additional child.

These inducements to raise large families, however, were not attractive enough to have much effect. The Quebec government also began to promote immigration from other countries. Quebec was the first province to create a Department of Immigration and became the most active of all provinces in encouraging immigration. It remains the province with the most comprehensive immigration agreements signed with the federal government. The most recent, the Canada-Quebec Accord of 1991, allows Quebec to use its own system for evaluating potential immigrants—one that gives points for language as well as education and job experience.

At the end of the twentieth century, the fastest growing group of immigrants arriving in Quebec was Arab speakers, for whom French is often a second language. In the four decades prior, the main groups of immigrants came from China, Vietnam, Cambodia, Haiti, and various South American countries, especially Chile, very few of them being French speaking. In 1974, Quebec attempted to limit the influx of non-French-speaking immigrants by passing Bill 22, requiring the children of immigrants be enrolled in French-language schools.

■ *Vietnamese immigrants upon arrival in Montreal in 1977. Many immigrants to Quebec eventually leave the region.*

In any case, the new immigrants did not do much to stem the province's slowing population growth, since many of them, after becoming Canadian citizens, either moved on to neighboring provinces or to the United States. According to one report, more than three-hundred thousand of the half-million immigrants who came to Quebec between 1969 and 1990 left the province to seek their fortunes elsewhere. Another report says that between 1983 and 1992, 25 percent of Quebec's immigrants left within ten years of arriving. Whatever the actual numbers, they show a significant drain.

The Flight of the English-Speaking Minority

Another group has been leaving Quebec in recent years: the English-speaking minority. In part this has been in response to the ongoing separatist movement, which if it were successful would presumably make the French-speaking majority even more dominant. The Quebecois-controlled provincial government has, since the Parti Quebecois first swept into power in 1976, passed a number of laws that have annoyed or alienated the province's Anglophones. Many of these laws were meant to protect the primacy of French language and culture. The most notable, Bill 101, was passed in 1977. It made French the province's only official language and, in effect, attempted to ban all English (and even bilingual) commercial and road signs.

By 1990, Quebec was spending tens of millions of dollars annually on various government agencies dealing with "language problems," including the renaming of English town, river, and mountain names into French. Undercover inspectors were also sent to inspect shops for any non-French signs and to check that the salespeople greeted their customers in French. Violations could result in court appearances and fines of up to $570.

As a result, English-speaking families and firms began to leave the province, further weakening its economic and political power. A joke among the English-speaking population was "101 or 401," with the latter referring to the main highway route south from Montreal to Toronto, Ontario. Population statistics suggest that since the mid-1960s more than 600,000 Quebecers have left the province, either for other provinces, the United States, or other countries. The size of this exodus is unmatched by any other Canadian province. It is not known exactly how many of these ex-Quebecers are English speaking, but officials estimate that at least two-thirds are— some 400,000 people. Moreover, many of these English speak-

■ *Toronto (pictured)
has recently surpassed
Montreal as the wealthi-
est and most populous
city in Canada.*

ers are among the province's young professional class. The
older English speakers who have remained behind generate
less income, need more social services—and are not having
any children.

Large corporations have also departed, often leaving
Montreal or Quebec City for nearby Toronto. In the early
1960s Montreal was the largest city in Canada. In recent years
it has been surpassed in wealth and population by Toronto.

Reversing the Plight of the First Nations

The First Nations' trials to survive as an important voice in
Quebec have been much more desperate compared to English
speakers. The partnership relationship based on the fur trade
between the First Nations and some of the earliest Europeans
did not last long. By the mid-eighteenth century, colonial
governments were negotiating treaties requiring First Nations
tribes to give up much of their land in return for the right to
live on reserves. In many cases these reserves were far from
tribes' ancestral lands, and located in areas that made it difficult for tribes to survive through hunting and fishing. This
was true across all the Canadian provinces (and similar to the
fate of Native Americans). In some parts of Canada during
the mid-twentieth century, provincial governments tried to
ban Indians' traditional practices and even removed Indian
children from reservations to be placed in boarding schools.

■ *An Indian camp in northwest Quebec. Approximately 67,000 First Nations people reside in the province of Quebec.*

These boarding schools taught only white culture and forbade the Indian children from speaking their own language.

But then the Quebec government began to lead the way in returning rights to the Indians. In 1960 they were given the right to vote. In 1985 the Quebec government became the first in Canada to recognize the aboriginal nations and their right to govern themselves. Some tribes began to receive money in exchange for development rights, such as for hydroelectricity. That meant the Indians were finally free to practice their own culture, speak and teach their children their own language, and follow their own traditions. They could own and control land, hunt, fish, and farm as they wanted, and decide how they wanted to prosper.

Today, First Nations peoples make up one in every hundred residents of Quebec, and the quality of their lives is improving as they are freed from government control and suppression of their culture. Despite recent improvements, Indian poverty is still widespread today. Some 52,000 of the First Nations people live in 54 communities around the province, and the remaining 15,000 live among the general populace, mainly in the Montreal area. They generally communicate using their native language and speak French or English as a second language. Politically their communities are run through band councils led by the chief.

■ First Nations Survivors

The many First Nations tribes in Quebec have different beliefs and customs but most fall into one of two language groups that have inhabited Quebec since precolonial times. The Abenaki, Algonquin, Attikamek, Cree, Malecite, Mi'kmaq, Montagnais, and Naskapi are part of the Algonquian culture. The Huron-Wendat and Mohawk are part of the Iroquoian culture. The Inuit in the far north of Quebec, formerly called Eskimos, are a distinct culture with different origins. As can be seen from the chart below, some nations have very few members and two have lost their language entirely. But considering all the challenges they have faced over the centuries, it is perhaps amazing that these nations have survived at all.

Nation	Number of individuals in Quebec Province	Percent speaking their language
Abenaki	1,890	3%
Algonquin	7,980	60%
Attikamek	4,900	98%
Cree	12,430	100%
Huron-Wendat	2,790	0%
Malecite	570	0%
Mi'kmaq	4,375	40%
Mohawk	14,735	15%
Montagnais	13,775	80%
Naskapi	570	100%

By taking action to improve the lives of the 67,000 First Nations people in the province, the Quebec government has gone a long way to address a problem that other Canadian provinces and U.S. states still have to resolve. But a long way remains to go to restore the once proud and able First Nations peoples to the strong communities that had survived for so many thousands of years in the harsh environment that is Quebec. A major hurdle is unemployment, which in most native communities ranges from 50 to 80 percent.

Juggling Environment, Jobs, and Land Rights

If ever there were a beautiful environment that deserved protection, it is the expansive wilds of Quebec. With so many Quebecers out enjoying the countryside, and tourism generating

■ Quebec Lobbies for the World Environment

In recent years the people of Quebec have begun to realize that their beautiful forests were suffering from the effects of pollution drifting north from American factories. As a result, Quebecers have taken the lead in promoting the idea that Earth is an interconnected system and that environmental protections need to be worldwide in focus. The Quebec government has consistently been one of the first to propose or support international agreements to protect the environment and essential resources. Examples include the Montreal Protocol on Substances That Deplete the Ozone Layer, the Agenda 21 program, the Convention on Biological Diversity, and the United Nations Framework Convention on Climate Change.

Setting a good example in their backyard, Quebecers have implemented many programs to reduce or prevent pollution and to clean up contaminated areas. One example is the adaptation of the Quebec-invented snowmaker to treat wastewater and so return it purified to the environment. Specially adapted units can also be used to treat contaminated water generated by the many mines in the province, thereby not only removing from the environment 90 percent of the metals in the water but also recovering them for use by the mining companies.

As a result of its strong stand on environmental issues, Quebec has become the place of choice for international seminars and conferences on the environment, as well as home to many environmental organizations, including the Secretariat of the United Nations Convention on Biological Diversity, the E7 Network of Expertise for the Global Environment, and the Secretariat of the International Program on Chemical Safety of the World Health Organization.

■ *Protesters march in Quebec to demonstrate against environmental destruction.*

■ *A hydroelectric power plant on Quebec's La Grande River.*

important revenue for the province, the need to protect the province's land, air, and water from pollution is widely recognized. As in many other industrialized societies, however, respect for the environment faces competition from those who argue that jobs, and even First Nations' rights, are more important.

In Quebec one of the main crossroads for these competing interests is the issue of development of vast expanses of land in central and northern Quebec for hydroelectric power. Hydroelectric development begun in the 1960s by Hydro-Quebec, the huge province-run monopoly, led to a vast area of west-central Quebec being flooded by dams. These dams more than doubled the province's energy output, however, allowing Quebec to power its industries and even export energy.

Some of the flooded lands were claimed by the native Cree as ancestral homeland. In 1975, Hydro-Quebec and the Cree signed an agreement to build a second stage of dams and power plants on the La Grande River, which empties into the James Bay. The agreement soon broke down and halted further development. Lawsuits were filed by both sides, and the Cree started an effective public relations campaign to paint Quebec as unconcerned for native rights.

Only recently has the impasse been resolved. In 2001, Ted Moses, Grand Chief of the Grand Council of the Cree (Quebec), met with newly elected Quebec premier Bernard Landry and hammered out an agreement to end the long-standing land dispute. In a series of referenda in early 2002, a 70 percent majority of the province's Cree approved the historic treaty. It opens up more of their huge territory to mining, logging, and further industrial development by Hydro-Quebec, but will pay the Cree at least $3.5 billion over fifty years. The Cree will have a say in where dams are placed, and they hope to protect some of their most sacred traditional hunting and trapping holdings. Even though the monetary payment is huge, the agreement worked out was controversial among the Cree, many of whom argued against it on cultural and environmental terms.

Competing in the Canadian— and Global—Economy

Just as the environment is increasingly being recognized as an interconnected jigsaw, the economies of the world have grown more and more intertwined as travel and communication become faster and easier. Like other regions, Quebec finds itself suddenly having to adapt to new ways of doing business.

■ Ontario's Economy Surpassing Quebec's

Quebec and its mostly Anglophone neighbor to the west share some similarities, placing either first or second among Canada's ten provinces in such factors as land size, population, and economic output. The two provinces also have somewhat similar stores of natural resources, such as lumber and hydroelectric potential, and are sited along waterways that allow for extensive trade-related business. Given the similarities, it is noteworthy that Ontario seems to be increasingly prosperous compared to Quebec.

The unemployment rate for Quebec in 2001 was almost 12 percent, more than double the rate in the United States overall but only slightly higher than Canada as a whole (approximately 10 percent). Quebec's rate was lower than the harder-hit maritime provinces (Newfoundland's 25 percent was the highest rate in Canada) but higher than the prairie provinces, and significantly higher than Ontario (at 9 percent).

Quebec's overall economy has also suffered recently in comparison to Ontario. As analyst Matthew Stevenson noted about the gross domestic products of the two provinces, "The two are very similar in the mid-1960s, but begin to diverge dramatically in later periods. Both provinces experienced similar stagnation and decline in the recession of the early 1990s, but since then, Ontario has shown dramatic growth in contrast to Quebec."

Stevenson and others have pointed to a number of factors that may help to explain the economy's relative demise, including the brain drain of

Instead of Canada, or a powerful United States, dictating how business and trade are to be carried out, Quebecers find themselves complying with the rules of the World Trade Organization (WTO) and its more than 130 members. The WTO grew out of a desire after World War II to create international institutions that could promote trade and economic cooperation between countries. As such, it has formulated rules that member countries agree to follow when trading with one another. In some cases, these rules can conflict with laws made by elected governments.

One example is Quebec's fashion industry. As a result of decisions made by the WTO, after 2003 Quebec will no longer be protected from foreign competition with cheaper products produced by low-wage employees in less-developed nations. For the most part, Quebecers are viewing this development as a challenge. Instead of making clothes for all of Quebec, they will make clothes for the whole world. And they will use their

■ *Although similar to Quebec in many ways, the province of Ontario (pictured) has enjoyed greater economic growth than its neighbor.*

young (mostly English-speaking) professionals, higher taxes in Quebec compared to Ontario, and uncertainties about Quebec's future status as a province or a nation.

well-trained workforce to produce something that the lower-paid foreign workers are not producing: high-quality, more-expensive products for those who prefer fine clothing. In this way, everybody wins. For Quebec to do well, therefore, it will have to restore stability for the individual in the workplace, and find a way to help the majority of its companies succeed and expand in the new global economy.

To Stay or Not to Stay

Although separation from Canada is not the fervent issue among Quebecois that it once was, it remains not fully resolved. Following Premier Levesque's failed attempt via the 1980 referendum to separate Quebec from Canada, the movement to keep Quebec within the country was dealt a setback with the failure of the Meech Lake Accord. This agreement, orchestrated in 1987 by then Canadian prime minister Brian Mulroney, would have officially recognized Quebec's uniqueness within the Canadian Federation. It would also have given the province certain guarantees, such as ensuring that one-third of the Supreme Court judges will be selected from it and that it be granted a veto over constitutional amendments. The accord was not ratified by the 1990 deadline. A similar agreement, the Charlottetown Accord of 1992, was rejected by six of ten provinces in a national referendum.

■ *Quebecois show their support for separation from Canada.*

The separatist effort gained renewed momentum from the unwillingness of the country at large to officially acknowledge Quebec's unique status within Canada. In 1995, under the leadership of Jacques Parizeau, Quebec's premier and leader of the Parti Quebecois, Quebec held another referendum on separation. The measure failed by a mere 1 percent of votes cast. Not surprisingly, 90 percent of English-speaking and immigrant Quebecers voted against separation, and almost 60 percent of Francophones voted for it. The results showed that the majority of French speakers in Quebec still wanted to separate.

Since then, a major legal decision has muddied the waters of separation. In 1998 the Canadian Supreme Court ruled that Quebec could not separate from Canada without negotiating with the federal government and the other provinces. And today, although Quebec's premier Landry strongly favors separatism, the issue faces an uphill battle.

A prominent concern confronting Quebecers who favor separation from Canada relates to Quebec's shrinking share of the national wealth, which then reduces its political influence in Canada. The other provinces, in other words, are not as concerned anymore with a province that is increasingly less powerful and that continues to search for a solution to a problem others do not see as all that important.

■ *Most of Quebec's younger generation are not in favor of separation.*

Perhaps most disturbing for proseparatists, the issue seems not to resonate with young Quebecois. As Quebec writer Benoit Aubin has noted:

> For decades, the separatists' doctrine was that Quebec could not develop as a "nation" unless it became independent from Ottawa—or, failing that, without acquiring a significant share of extra constitutional powers. But to this day, that dogma has proven to be a hard sell. Quebecers, especially the younger generations, have rejected the nationalist politics and the constitutional wranglings of the past—now widely perceived as a sterile baby boom thing. Instead, they have gone resolutely multicultural and global. And, to the separatists' dismay, being part of Canada has not been an impediment.[15]

A History of Compromise

Throughout history, the people of Quebec have generally tried to find ways for different groups to cooperate and live together. This has been true of the French trappers with the Amerindians as well as the British with the French. Canada itself, with Quebec for centuries its most influential part, embraces compromise. Unlike many other large countries, it has not experienced any military revolution, significant civil war, or the violent overthrow of any government in order to become and remain a country.

The Canadians tend to be practical in their view of life, as if the demands of surviving in the wilderness have taught them that the real enemy is not the other person, but one's own possible ignorance and intolerance that may cause one to do irrational things. Time and again, Quebecers have avoided armed confrontation and instead looked for a compromise solution that still respects the rights of others. This tendency to want to find compromises is recognized around the world as something of value as countries interact more and more in the global economy, and they look to Canadians to help settle their disagreements—whether about trade, land, politics, or the environment.

Quebec clearly has many challenges to tackle if it is to continue as a prosperous province. Given the vast natural resources, the almost unlimited power available, its strong traditions and culture, as well as the new perspectives of immigrants, there is no reason the province cannot surmount these challenges.

Facts About Quebec

Government
- Form: parliamentary system with federal and provincial levels
- Highest official: premier, who administers provincial legislation and regulations
- Capital: Quebec City
- Entered confederation: July 1, 1867 (one of the original four provinces)
- Provincial flag: the Fleurdelisé, four fleurs-de-lis on a blue background with a white cross
- Motto: "Je me souviens" (I remember)

Land
- Area: 594,860 square miles (1,540,680 square kilometers); 15.5% of total land of Canada; largest province
- Boundaries: bounded on the north by Hudson Strait and Ungava Bay; on the east by the Labrador area of Newfoundland and the Gulf of St. Lawrence; on the south by New Brunswick and the states of Maine, New Hampshire, Vermont, and New York; and on the south and west by Ontario, James Bay, and Hudson Bay
- Bordering bodies of water: Ungava Bay, Hudson Strait, Hudson Bay, James Bay, Ottawa River, St. Lawrence River, Gulf of St. Lawrence
- National parks: Forillon, Mingan Archipelago, La Mauricie, Saguenay-St. Lawrence
- Provincial parks: 17 as of 1995, encompassing 1,641 square miles (4,249 square kilometers); also 26 wildlife reserves
- Highest point: Mont d'Iberville in the Torngat Mountains, 5,420 feet (1,652 meters)

- Largest lake: Mistassini, 900 square miles (2,336 square kilometers)
- Other major lakes: St. Jean, Bienville, Payne, Clearwater
- Longest river: St. Lawrence, 750 miles (1,200 kilometers), including portion in Ontario
- Other major rivers: St. Mauricie, Gatineau, Harricana, Caniapiskau, Ottawa
- Time zones: Eastern Standard Time
- Geographical extremes: 45°N to 62°30'N latitude; 79°30'W to 57°W longitude

Climate

- Coldest day: −38° F (−39° C) around Hull on December 29, 1933
- Greatest number of consecutive days with highest temperature above 90° F (32° C): 11, starting June 27, 1946, in Nominingue
- Highest hourly average wind speed: 126 mph (201 km/h) at Cape Hopes Advance, Ungava Peninsula, on November 18, 1931 (Canadian record)

People

- Population: 7,237,479 (2001 census); second-highest population of provinces and territories; 24.1% of Canada's total population of 30,007,094
- Annual growth rate: 1.4% from 1996 to 2001 (fifth-highest among provinces and territories)
- Density: 5 persons per square kilometer (Canadian national average: 3)
- Location: 78.4% urban, 21.6% rural; only 35,000 people live in northern Quebec, which makes up 70% of Quebec's total area
- Predominant heritages: French, British, aboriginal
- Largest ethnic groups: Italians, Portuguese, Haitians, Lebanese, South Americans, Southeast Asians
- Major religious groups: Catholics, Protestants, Jews, Muslims
- Primary languages: 81% French, 8% English, 11% other; approximately 90 percent of the population is bilingual
- Largest metropolitan areas: Montreal, population 3,426,350, an increase of 3.0% between 1996 and 2001; second-largest metro area in Canada; Quebec City, 682,757, seventh-largest
- Other major cities: Hull, Verdun, Laval, Sherbrooke, Trois Rivieres
- Life expectancy at birth, 3-year average 1995–1997: men 74.6 years; women 81.0; total both sexes 77.9, sixth among provinces and territories (Canadian average: men 75.4; women 81.2)

- Infant mortality rate in 1996: 4.6 per 1,000 live births, lowest rate among provinces and territories
- Immigration 7/1/2000–6/30/2001: 36,664, 14.5% of Canadian total of 252,088; third-highest of provinces and territories
- Births 7/1/2000–6/30/2001: 71,463
- Deaths 7/1/2000–6/30/2001: 53,419
- Marriages in 1998: 23,746
- Divorces in 1998: 16,916

Plants and animals
- Provincial bird: Snowy owl
- Provincial flower: White garden lily
- Provincial tree: Yellow birch
- Endangered, threatened, or vulnerable species: 92, including four-toed salamander, spotted turtle, woodland caribou, lynx, mountain lion, golden eagle, bald eagle, peregrine falcon, great gray owl, striped bass, Atlantic and lake sturgeons

Holidays
- National: January 1 (New Year's Day); Good Friday; Easter; Easter Monday; Monday preceding May 25 (Victoria or Dollard Day); July 1 or, if this date falls on a Sunday, July 2 (Canada's birthday); 1st Monday of September (Labour Day); 2nd Monday of October (Thanksgiving); November 11 (Remembrance Day); December 25 (Christmas); December 26 (Boxing Day)
- Provincial: January 2; June 24 (Quebec National Day or Saint-Jean-Baptiste Day)

Economy
- Gross domestic product per capita: $26,432 in 1999, fifth among provinces and territories and 78.1% compared to U.S. average[16]
- Gross provincial product: $215 billion at market prices in 2000, second among the provinces and territories and 21.2% of gross national product
- Major exports: energy (from hydroelectric production; also petroleum), forest products, minerals, food and beverage products, fish, manufactured goods
- Agriculture: dairy, vegetables, potatoes, hay
- Tourism: cultural and recreational attractions year-round; skiing and other winter sports, fishing, boating, hiking
- Logging: pulp, paper, lumber
- Manufacturing: aluminum, clothing, furniture, chemicals, paper products, steel, space and aeronautics, pharmaceuticals, telecommunications
- Mining: copper, iron, zinc, silver, gold, asbestos, nickel

Notes

Introduction: What Is Quebec?

1. **Quebec's Government Portal,** "Historical Overview." www.gouv.qc.ca

Chapter 1: A Rich and Challenging Land

2. Quoted in Reader's Digest, *Heritage of Canada: Our Storied Past—and Where to Find It.* Montreal: The Reader's Digest Association (Canada) Limited, 1978, p. 77.

Chapter 2: The First Nations and European Pioneers

3. Quoted in Reader's Digest, *Heritage of Canada,* p. 36.

4. Reader's Digest, *Heritage of Canada,* p. 34.

5. Quoted in Edgar A. Collard, *Montreal: The Days That Are No More.* Toronto: Doubleday Canada Limited, 1976, p. 5.

6. Quoted in Editors of Time-Life Books, *Canada.* Alexandria, VA: Time-Life Books, 1988, p. 49.

Chapter 3: The French and British Struggle for Power

7. Quoted in Collard, *Montreal: The Days That Are No More*, p. 110.

8. Quoted in Collard, *Montreal: The Days That Are No More*, p. 109.

9. Quoted in "Report of Lord Durham on the Affairs of British North America," Documents in Quebec History, Quebec History, *Marianopolis College*, www2.marianopolis.edu.

Chapter 4: Life in Quebec Today
10. André Desnoyers and Yves Lirette, "The Knowledge-Based Economy and the Labour Market," *Human Resources Development Canada.* www.qc.hrdc-drhc.gc.ca.

Chapter 5: A Culture Alive
11. Mark Fellows, "The Apocalypse of Jack Kerouac: Meditations on the 30th Anniversary of His Death," *Culture Wars*, November 1999. www.culturewars.com.
12. Quoted in Canadian Press, "Reactions to Richler's Death," July 4, 2001.
13. Quoted in "Friends and Colleagues Remember Mordecai Richler," *Bravo!Canada.* www.bravo.ca.
14. Quoted in Reader's Digest, *Heritage of Canada,* p. 255.

Chapter 6: Looking for Solutions
15. Benoit Aubin, "Where the Solitudes Meet," *Macleans*, December 31, 2001.

Facts About Quebec
16. *Demographia,* "Canada: Regional Gross Domestic Product Data 1999." www.demographia.com.

Chronology

Circa 8000 B.C.   The land that will later become Quebec is first inhabited by Inuit and other First Nations.

1534   Jacques Cartier lands on the Gaspé Peninsula and claims the surrounding land for France.

1535–1536   Cartier explores the St. Lawrence River and lands at the sites that later become the cities of Quebec and Montreal.

1608   Samuel de Champlain lands at the future site of Quebec City and builds a fur-trading post.

1620s   Jesuit missionaries come to the area to try to convert natives to Christianity.

1630s   Epidemics break out among the Huron and other First Nations people.

1642   A permanent settlement is established at the mission of Ville-Marie, the future site of Montreal.

1649   Following Iroquois attacks, the Jesuits abandon St. Marie.

1650s   The "coureurs de bois" become active in the fur trade.

1663   The king of France takes charge of "New France," sending troops to defend the colony and encouraging settlement.

1667   The French force the Iroquois to make peace.

1670 The king of England grants the Hudson's Bay Company a charter to trade in fur throughout all territories surrounding Hudson Bay, including much of present-day Quebec.

1689–1701 Fierce fighting between the French and England's allies, the Iroquois.

1689–1748 A series of wars between France and the rest of Europe spreads to Canada.

1701 French and Iroquois agree to a peace, which is never broken.

1759 British troops under General Wolfe defeat French troops under General Montcalm in the Battle of the Plains of Abraham outside Quebec City, in effect ending New France as a French colony.

1760 The French formally surrender to the British at Montreal.

1763 France's signing of the Treaty of Paris gives all of mainland Canada to the British; the people of New France are forced to accept "La Conquest" and become a British colony.

1774 The Quebec Act passed by the British Parliament reinstates French civil law and allows the French to practice their own language and religion.

1775–1776 The French in Quebec help the British drive out an American invading force during the American Revolutionary War.

1791 The Constitutional Act establishes the British parliamentary system in Canada and gives French Canadians the right to vote; it also divides the country into mainly English-speaking Upper Canada (present-day Ontario) with York (Toronto) as its capital, and French-speaking Lower Canada (Quebec).

1812–1814 Another American invasion of Canada fails during a brief war between the United States and the British.

1837 An uprising in Upper and Lower Canada over misgovernment by British elites is put down by the army; Britain sends Lord Durham to investigate and his report recommends reuniting Upper and Lower Canada and increasing their independence from Great Britain.

1840 The Act of Union unites the provinces of Upper and Lower Canada.

1867 The British North America Act creates the Dominion of Canada, a confederation of Ontario, Quebec, Nova Scotia, and New Brunswick.

1917 French Canadian–led protests against conscription during World War I divide the country.

1940 Women are allowed to vote for the first time in Quebec.

1960s The "Quiet Revolution" modernizes Quebec and weakens the hold of the Roman Catholic Church over day-to-day affairs.

1967 Montreal hosts Expo 67 in celebration of Canada's 100th birthday.

1968 Pierre Trudeau becomes prime minister of Canada; René Levesque, a Quebec journalist, forms the Parti Quebecois with a platform to separate Quebec from the rest of Canada.

1970 Terrorists of the Front de Liberation du Québec (FLQ) kidnap a British diplomat and Quebec minister; after the FLQ murders the minister, the Trudeau government proclaims martial law and cracks down on the FLQ, eventually breaking up the organization.

1976 The Parti Quebecois wins the Quebec Provincial Elections; the Summer Olympic Games are staged in Montreal.

1980 By a significant margin, the people of Quebec vote in a referendum against separation from the rest of Canada.

1982 Canada adopts a new constitution in the face of outspoken Quebecois opposition, sparking a decade of increasing strife between French- and English-speaking Canadians.

1985 UNESCO names Quebec City a World Heritage City.

1990 The Meech Lake Accord offers promise of compromise and recognition of Quebec as a distinct society within Canada but is never approved by provincial governments.

1993 Quebec-born Jean Chrétien elected prime minister of Canada.

1995 By a slim 1 percent margin, Quebecers again vote in a referendum to reject separation from Canada.

2001 Parti Quebecois leader Bernard Landry is elected premier of Quebec.

For Further Reading

Craig Brown, ed., *The Illustrated History of Canada.* Toronto: Key Porter Books, 1997. Seven historians take the reader through Canadian history from 1534 to the 1980s, presenting facts, tidbits about everyday life, and the bigger picture in an easy read.

Hugh Durnford, ed., *Heritage of Canada.* Montreal: The Reader's Digest Association (Canada), 1978. A fascinating account of Canadian history, with many stories and pictures.

Editors of Time-Life Books, *Canada.* Alexandria, VA: Time-Life Books, 1988. A pictorial essay of people in modern Canada.

Editors of Time-Life Books, with text by Ogden Tanner, *The Canadians.* Alexandria, VA: Time-Life Books, 1977. Although the book focuses on the opening up of the Canadian West, it also covers the early history of the Quebec-based explorers.

Linda Ferguson, *Canada.* New York: Charles Scribner's Sons, 1979. A good basic book for students interested in reading about the history, geography, and people of Canada.

John F. Grabowski, *Canada.* San Diego, CA: Lucent Books, 1998. An informative and readable introduction to the country as part of the publisher's Modern Nations of the World series.

William Howarth, *Traveling the Trans-Canada.* Washington, DC: National Geographic Society, 1987. A wonderful pictorial essay of life in Canada at the end of the last century.

Works Consulted

Books

Lawrence Burpee, *The Discovery of Canada.* Toronto: Macmillan, 1944. Exciting stories of the earliest Europeans to explore Canada, starting with the Vikings and based on firsthand accounts.

Edgar A. Collard, *Montreal: The Days That Are No More.* Toronto: Doubleday Canada Limited, 1976. A dozen vignettes covering the history of Montreal, showing its colorful character and the stories behind the events.

Steven Leacock, *Canada: Foundations of Its Future.* Montreal: privately printed, 1941. A history of Canada from the beginning of the nineteenth century onward.

Andrew H. Malcolm, *The Canadians.* New York: St. Martin's Press, 1992. A personal view of Canada and Canadians by the Canadian Bureau Chief of *The New York Times.*

Kenneth McNaught, *The Penguin History of Canada.* London: Penguin Books, 1988. A short history written by a professor.

Michelin Quebec. Greenville, SC: Michelin Travel Publications, 1996. This entry in the famous Green Guide series offers detailed background information on destinations throughout the province.

Jan Morris, *O Canada.* New York: HarperCollins, 1990. Penetrating insights from an astute observer of Canada's unique society and culture.

Desmond Morton, *A Short History of Canada.* Toronto: McClelland & Stewart, 1997. An informative and factual history suitable for students.

Peter Newman, *Company of Adventurers.* Toronto: Penguin Books Canada, 1985. Stories about and history of the fur trade that opened up Canada.

Frederick Pratson, *A Guide to Eastern Canada.* Old Saybrook, CT: Globe Pequot Press, 1998. An interesting tourist guide.

Reader's Digest, *Heritage of Canada: Our Storied Past—and Where to Find It.* Montreal: The Reader's Digest Association (Canada) Limited, 1978. Interesting background and anecdotes on places and characters.

Mordecai Richler, *Oh Canada, Oh Québec.* New York: Alfred A. Knopf, 1992. A humorous look at the separatist movement.

Roger Riendeau, *A Brief History of Canada.* Markham, Ont.: Fitzhenry & Whiteside, 2000. A complete history of Canada to the present day.

John Saywell, *Canada: Pathways to the Present.* Toronto: Stoddard Publishing, 1999. A concise account of Canada's history, geography, politics, and economics.

George Woodcock, *Canada and the Canadians.* Harrisburg, PA: Stackpole Books, 1970. The history and life of Canada up to the mid-twentieth century, focusing on politics, culture, and the urbanization of the country.

Periodicals

Benoit Aubin, "Where the Solitudes Meet," *Macleans,* December 31, 2001. "Reactions to Richler's Death," Canadian Press, July 4, 2001.

Internet Sources

Bravo!Canada, "Friends and Colleagues Remember Mordecai Richler." www.bravo.ca.

Demographia, "Canada: Regional Gross Domestic Product Data: 1999." www.demographia.com.

André Desnoyers and Yves Lirette, "The Knowledge-Based Economy and the Labour Market," *Human Resources Development Canada.* www.qc.hrdc-drhc.gc.ca.

Mark Fellows, "The Apocalypse of Jack Kerouac: Meditations on the 30th Anniversary of His Death," *Culture Wars,* November 1999. www.culturewars.com.

Marianopolis College, Documents in Quebec History, "Report of Lord Durham on the Affairs of Brittish North America." www2.marianopolis.edu.

Websites

Canadian Statistics (www.statcan.ca). A useful array of facts and statistics on Canada, including Quebec.

Natural History of Quebec (www.redpathmuseum.mcgill.ca). Provides information on the geology and vegetation zones of Quebec.

Quebec: WorldWeb Travel Guide (www.quebec.worldweb.com). An easy-to-read tourism guide.

Quebec's Government Portal (www.gouv.qc.ca). The province's official website offers information on tourism, the economy, institutions, culture, and more.

Index

Picture Credits

About the Author

Steven Ferry has written and photographed for various U.S. publishers and corporations. He has authored over a dozen books, including several for middle schoolers.